CAMPAIGN 354

KING PHILIP'S WAR 1675–76

America's Deadliest Colonial Conflict

GABRIELE ESPOSITO   ILLUSTRATED BY GIUSEPPE RAVA

Series editor Nikolai Bogdanovic

OSPREY PUBLISHING
Bloomsbury Publishing Plc
PO Box 883, Oxford, OX1 9PL, UK
1385 Broadway, 5th Floor, New York, NY 10018, USA
E-mail: info@ospreypublishing.com
www.ospreypublishing.com

OSPREY is a trademark of Osprey Publishing Ltd

First published in Great Britain in 2020

A catalog record for this book is available from the British Library.

ISBN: PB 9781472842978; eBook 9781472842985; ePDF 9781472842954;
XML 9781472842961

20 21 22 23 24   10 9 8 7 6 5 4 3 2 1

Maps by Bounford.com
3D BEVs by Paul Kime
Index by Alison Worthington
Typeset by PDQ Digital Media Solutions, Bungay, UK
Printed and bound in India by Replika Press Private Ltd.

Artist's note

Readers may care to note that the original paintings from which the color
plates in this book were prepared are available for private sale. All
reproduction copyright whatsoever is retained by the publishers. The
illustrator can be contacted via the following email address:

info@g-rava.it

The publishers regret that they can enter into no correspondence upon
this matter.

A note on photographic images

Thanks are due to Kenneth Grant, Eric B. Schultz, Watertown Free Public
Library, and the Barrington Land Conservation Trust for permitting the use
of their images in this work.

Osprey Publishing supports the Woodland Trust, the UK's leading woodland
conservation charity.

To find out more about our authors and books visit
www.ospreypublishing.com. Here you will find extracts, author
interviews, details of forthcoming events and the option to sign up for
our newsletter.

Author's acknowledgements

Special thanks are due to Nikolai Bogdanovic, for supporting the project of
this book from the outset and for helping me with his precious advice.
Another special acknowledgement goes to Giuseppe Rava, for the
magnificent color plates that illustrate this title: his beautiful artwork has
brought the clashes of King Philip's War to life once again. Thanks also to
the excellent reenactment group Henricus Citie Militia and in particular
Dennis Strawderman. Last but not least, I want to express my deep
gratitude to Eric B. Schultz, the author of a key study on King Philip's War,
who has changed the general perception of this conflict.

Dedication

To my parents Maria Rosaria and Benedetto, for their immense love and
fundamental support.

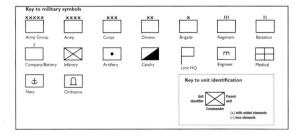

PREVIOUS PAGE
The Siege of Brookfield. (Public domain)

CONTENTS

ORIGINS OF THE CAMPAIGN 5

The settlement of New England . The Great Migration and new settlements . Epidemics
Military cooperation between the colonies . Rising tensions . The rise of Metacomet
The path to war

CHRONOLOGY 24

OPPOSING COMMANDERS 26

Native American . Colonist

OPPOSING FORCES 29

Native American . Colonist . Native American allies

OPPOSING PLANS 38

Native American . Colonist

THE CAMPAIGN 42

The Raid on Swansea and the opening attacks . Wheeler's Surprise and the Siege of Brookfield
The war spreads . The Northern Theater: Maine . Deerfield, Northfield, and Beers' Ambush
The Battle of Bloody Brook . The Siege of Springfield and the attack on Hatfield
The Great Swamp Fight . The intervention of the Mohawks . The Lancaster Raid and the attack on Medfield
The attacks on Northampton and Marlborough . Pierce's Fight . Further attacks, March–April 1676
The capture of Canonchet . The Sudbury Fight . The Battle of Turner's Falls . The Attack on Hadley
Metacomet's death . The war in Maine

AFTERMATH 91

THE BATTLEFIELDS TODAY 92

BIBLIOGRAPHY 94

INDEX 95

New England in 1675

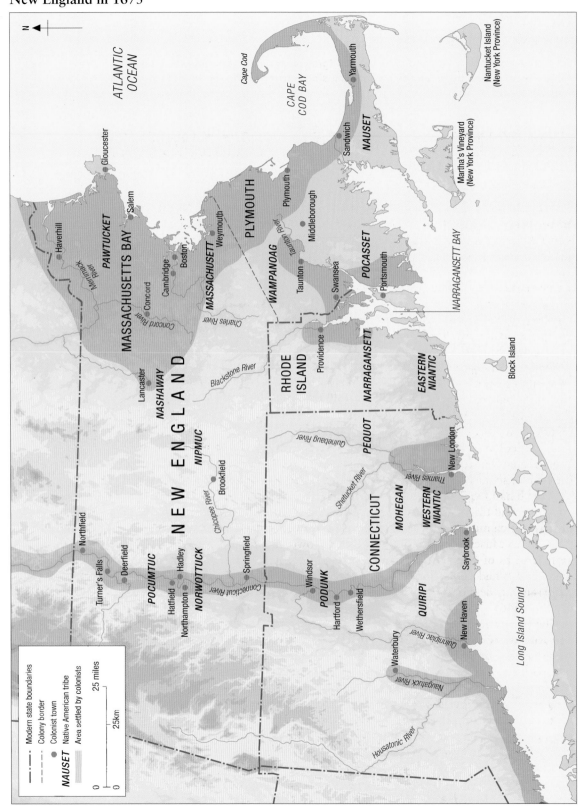

N

ATLANTIC OCEAN

Cape Cod

CAPE COD BAY

NAUSET

Nantucket Island (New York Province)

Gloucester

Salem

PAWTUCKET

Haverhill

Merrimack River

MASSACHUSETTS BAY

Concord

Cambridge

Boston

Concord River

MASSACHUSETT

Weymouth

Charles River

PLYMOUTH

Plymouth

Middleborough

Sandwich

Yarmouth

Martha's Vineyard (New York Province)

WAMPANOAG

Taunton River

Taunton

Swansea

POCASSET

Portsmouth

NARRAGANSETT BAY

Lancaster

NASHAWAY

NEW ENGLAND

Blackstone River

RHODE ISLAND

Providence

NARRAGANSETT

EASTERN NIANTIC

Block Island

NIPMUC

Brookfield

Chicopee River

Quinebaug River

PEQUOT

Shetucket River

MOHEGAN

Thames River

New London

WESTERN NIANTIC

Northfield

Turner's Falls

POCUMTUC

Deerfield

Hatfield

Hadley

Northampton

NORWOTTUCK

Springfield

Connecticut River

CONNECTICUT

Windsor

PODUNK

Hartford

Wethersfield

QUIRIPI

Saybrook

New Haven

Quinnipiac River

Waterbury

Naugatuck River

Long Island Sound

Housatonic River

Modern state boundaries
Colony border
Colonist town
NAUSET Native American tribe
Area settled by colonists

0   25 miles

0   25km

ORIGINS OF THE CAMPAIGN

King Philip's War was fought between the English colonists and Native Americans of New England. When it began in 1675, the English colonies in North America, then scattered in areas within a 1,000-mile-long section of the Atlantic coast, perceived themselves to be isolated entities. The colonists were a six- to eight-week-long sea voyage from England. Except for a shared sense of English identity, and at least nominal acknowledgement of the authority of the distant English crown, the colonies were separated and independent. Even the colonies in New England, which were clustered within a relatively small area, and whose settlers shared deeply held religious beliefs, each pursued their own interests.

The isolated English colonists were constantly imperiled. Natural disasters, crop failures, and epidemics of smallpox and other diseases were among the continuing dangers. Moreover, they faced military threats from two sources. The first were rival European powers—the French and the Dutch—who had ambitions in North America, and might at any time descend on a colony in force. The colonists had survived the Anglo-French War (1627–29); the First Anglo-Dutch War (1652–54); and the Second Anglo-Dutch War (1665–67). They had also survived the more recent Third Anglo-Dutch War, in which the French had fought as Dutch allies from 1672 to 1674.

The second threat came from the Native Americans. Most were in small nations, which might send raiders to attack colonists' homesteads, but were too weak to cause serious harm. There were, however, powerful permanent confederacies of Native American nations. One, the 30-nation Powhatan confederacy, had come close to annihilating the Virginia colonists before the Virginians destroyed it in wars from 1610 to 1614, 1622 to 1632, and 1644 to 1646.

The Native American nations also often formed temporary alliances for wars against common enemies. Such alliances, however, were difficult to form. Nations often refused to become allies of nations that had long been their enemies, and might soon be again.

Before 1675, such alliances always had been formed to fight Native American enemies. In 1675, however, Metacomet—called King Philip by the English—succeeded in creating the first that would fight the English colonists. The leader of the Wampanoags, a small New England nation, he persuaded several neighboring tribes to join his people in a war to drive them from New England.

Soon after they realized the scope of the peril they faced, the New England colonists learned that they would receive no help from England or the other English colonies. Aided only by their Native American allies, they then set aside their rivalries and disputes, and combined their forces for joint operations. That action by the New England colonies was the first step in a process of multi-colonial military cooperation that would reach its climax a century later, when all the English colonies would create an army to fight England in the Revolutionary War.

To prevail in King Philip's War, however, a united effort was not enough. Numbers alone would be insufficient against an enemy that would attack one of the scattered New England settlements, and then retire into the wilderness to prepare for an attack on another. The New England colonists had to study the art of fighting effectively in the woods. Taught by their Native American allies, they learned how to become lightly armed, highly mobile, and usually invisible warriors, who, fighting behind available cover, would deploy in masterful small-unit maneuvers. The frontiersman Benjamin Church formed a permanent unit of the best students, men that the colonists, using a contemporary synonym for foresters or gamekeepers, would call "rangers." Church's Rangers were the first in an American tradition of such units, which would include Rogers's Rangers in the French and Indian War, and the US Army Rangers today.

An early map of New England, representing the territory of Plymouth Colony, taken from William Wood's *New England's Prospect* (published in 1634). The latter served as a colonist's guide, and described the new American colonies to an audience of potential settlers. It contains much precious information on the early life of Plymouth Colony. (Public domain)

THE SETTLEMENT OF NEW ENGLAND

In 1607, the first English colony in America, Virginia, had been established at Jamestown, named for King James I of England. Thirteen years later, a second American colony appeared far to the north. The settlers, who called themselves the Pilgrims, were from a group of English Calvinists generally remembered as the Puritans. The Puritans would join those at Plymouth to settle at colonies in what they called New England. The New England colonies, shaped by the Puritans' religious faith, would be culturally very different from Virginia and other English colonies.

The Pilgrims had originally intended to settle near the Virginia colonists. They instead landed in 1620 in a harsher land. New England, as they named it, was bounded on the east and south by the Atlantic and Long Island Sound, and to the north and west by endless woods.

Far to the north, northwest, and west, the Puritans had powerful, and potentially dangerous, neighbors. To the north, in Maine, were the Sokoki and Androscoggin. They were the southernmost of the 27 nations often called the Abenaki peoples.

To the northwest were the five nations of the Mahican confederacy. Beyond the fierce Mahicans, were the Mohawks, who together with the Oneida, Onondaga, Cayuga, and Seneca, formed the five nations of the warlike Iroquois confederacy. To the west, along the Hudson River, were the Dutch settlements of New Netherland, surrounded by many small Native American nations. To the west beyond them, around the Delaware River, was the Munsee confederacy of about 20 nations. Further to the west, on the Susquehanna River, were the five nations of the powerful Susquehannock confederacy.

Nearer the Puritans were the Native American nations of New England. In the southwest, in Connecticut, was the powerful Pequot nation, which the Mohegans would soon leave to form their own tribe. There also were the Nashaways and other Nipmuc nations, who paid the Pequots tribute, and small, independent tribes like the Podunks. In the northwest, in western Massachusetts, were the Norwottucks and other nations of the Pocumtuc confederacy. In the southeast, in Rhode Island, were the nations of the Narragansett confederacy, and the Niantics, who paid them tribute. And to their north, in eastern Massachusetts, were the nations of the Wampanoag confederacy, and independent tribes like the Massachusetts.

Ever since his accession to the English and Irish thrones in 1603, James I had been pressed by requests for religious reform presented by the Puritan clergy. The king did not consider the Puritans highly, seeing them as extremists whose excessive requests could only harm the fragile stability of the Church of England. James' refusal to reform the religious institutions of the nation led to the birth of several Puritan movements that can collectively be described as "dissenting." The Puritans wished to live according to what was written in the Holy Bible, without making compromises for the dictats of any human authority. Consequently, these minor religious groups began to suffer persecution in several areas of England, and their position became tenuous and perilous. Their native country had very little to offer to them, and their evangelic zeal seemed impossible to express fully in what they considered to be an old and corrupt nation. They needed to find a new home, one in which they could live and worship without restrictions imposed by royal authority or prejudice.

In November 1620, a group of religious exiles known as the Pilgrims arrived in present-day Massachusetts on the ship *Mayflower*, seeking to establish a new colony. The Pilgrims held Calvinist religious beliefs similar to those of the Puritans, but, in contrast to them, believed their

A portrait of Edward Winslow, painted in 1651 in London. Winslow remains the only Pilgrim to have a verified portrait. He played an instrumental role in organizing the *Mayflower*'s journey to America, and his good relationships with the Wampanoag sachem Massasoit enabled the Pilgrims to receive crucial help in learning how to survive in the new land. (Public domain)

A page from William Bradford's journal *Of Plimoth Plantation*, written in 1646 and first printed in 1669. Bradford was governor of Plymouth Colony several times during the period 1621–57, and his journal is a key primary source for its history, particularly for the years 1621–46. *Of Plimoth Plantation* also contains a transcription of the famous Mayflower Compact, the first governing document of Plymouth Colony, signed on November 11, 1620—shown here. (Public domain)

congregation needed to be separated from the English state church. The Pilgrims were part of the Brownist English Dissenters, who had opted to abandon England on account of the religious persecution suffered, and had emigrated to the more tolerant Netherlands. Fearing the loss of their English cultural identity with the passing of time, they later decided to leave the Netherlands and seek a new home in the Americas. They collaborated with English investors to create a new settlement in North America, which was to be known as Plymouth Colony. Robert Cushman and John Carver were sent to England to obtain a land patent, but their negotiations were delayed because of internal disagreements within the London Company. Finally, a patent was secured by the Pilgrims' representatives in June 1619.

After a long period of preparation, and a difficult crossing of the Atlantic, the 102 Pilgrims that were embarked on the *Mayflower* finally sighted land on November 9, 1620. Several weeks later, on December 21, the colonists arrived at the site of what later became the settlement of Plymouth. During that winter, the Pilgrims suffered greatly from a lack of adequate shelter and through diseases such as scurvy. The 102 Pilgrim Fathers who had landed at Plymouth were humble people, accustomed to hard work and a Spartan lifestyle. In all that they did, the Pilgrims never doubted that they were carrying out the will of God. This resulted in a determination that enabled them to survive the first difficult years of settlement. Only 50 would survive the first winter out of the 102 who arrived on the *Mayflower*.

The military leader of Plymouth Colony from its outset was the Englishman Myles Standish, who had been hired by the Pilgrim Fathers. He had trained in military engineering at the University of Leiden and possessed a sound military knowledge. It was Standish who decided the defensive layout of the settlement soon after the colonists arrived at Plymouth. During the first winter in America, in February 1621, after several brief clashes with the local Native Americans, the male residents of the new colony were organized into military orders, with Standish as their captain. By the end of the month, a defensive position at Fort Hill had been completed, with the addition of five cannons landed from the *Mayflower*.

Contact with the local Native Americans up to this point had been only fleeting and sporadic. On March 16, 1621, a local Native American called Samoset, an Abenaki with basic English skills (which he learnt from fishermen visiting the Gulf of Maine), approached the colonists in Plymouth and established friendly relations. He returned a few days later with several other Native Americans, including one called Squanto, who had lived for

some time in England and could speak better English than Samoset. The Wampanoag Squanto had been taken prisoner by an English ship in 1614, and sold in Spain as a slave. He later converted to Christianity, was freed, and made his way to England, where he was assigned to an expedition to Newfoundland in Canada. From there, he managed to make his way back to his Wampanoag tribal territories.

At the meeting with Samoset and Squanto, the colonists learnt that the local leader was a Wampanoag chief named Massasoit, and a subsequent meeting with the chief was arranged. This bore good fruit, and a peace treaty was arranged between the colonists and Massasoit. According to its terms, settler and native would not bring harm on one another, and Massasoit would encourage his Native American tribal allies to enter peaceful negotiations with the New England settlers.

During the initial phase of colonial life, fur trading was the major source of income for colonists, who bought furs from the Native Americans and sold them into the European markets. Farming and agriculture were not particularly developed, remaining at a subsistence level. Relationships with the Native Americans continued to improve, notably after a mission was sent to Massasoit's tribal center to establish stronger commercial ties. The chief agreed an exclusive trading pact with the colonists, and promised to decline any further contact with French merchants, who were already active in the region.

Some tensions continued to exist between colonist and Native American. In August 1621, a sachem named Corbitant challenged Massasoit's

This 19th-century engraving by Albert Bobbettre shows the first meeting between the Pilgrim Fathers and the Wampanoag sachem Massasoit in 1621. From the outset, Massasoit sought to maintain positive relations with the colonists, and avoided violence. He understood that the colonists could be useful allies in his disputes with other Native American tribes. All this changed when Metacomet became sachem. (Library of Congress; public domain)

leadership and threatened an uprising against the colonial settlement. On August 14, 1621, Standish led a small force to capture or kill Corbitant, but Corbitant managed to flee his home village. The show of strength served its purpose, however, and in September, nine local sachems accompanied Corbitant to Plymouth, where a treaty of loyalty to King James was signed. In November 1621, Standish reinforced the protection of Plymouth Colony by encircling it with a stockade of logs, and strengthening the entrace gates. The stockade was completed by March 1622. The militia were also divided into four companies at this point, and were drilled to defend the settlement, with one company allocated to defend each side of the stockade. By this date, too, further settlers had started to arrive in New England—and more would soon follow.

THE GREAT MIGRATION AND NEW SETTLEMENTS

Following the accession of Charles I to the throne in 1625, religious conflict involving the Puritans worsened, and Parliament started to increasingly oppose royal authority. With the religious and political climates so hostile and threatening, many Puritans decided to leave the old country and move to New England. The success of Plymouth Colony encouraged them to send more expeditions and settlers to the New World, in order to form new communities where their faith could be freely practiced. This "Great Migration" would endure for two decades.

In 1630, after consolidation of the new colony at Salem, a flotilla of ships known as the Winthrop Fleet sailed from England for America with more than 700 Puritan colonists. The fleet arrived at Salem in June that year, marking the start of the most important phase of Puritan migration. Over the following ten years, a steady exodus of Puritans resulted from Old England, with some 10,000 people emigrating to Massachusetts and its neighboring colonies.

The advent of the English Civil War in the early 1640s brought a halt to Puritan migration, with a significant number of men returning to England to fight in the conflict. The colonial authorities of Massachusetts were generally sympathetic to the Parliamentary cause, and thus maintained positive relationships with Old England during the confused period of the English Commonwealth, and later under the Protectorate of Oliver Cromwell. In the years that followed, the economy of the colonies began to diversify and flourish: fur, tobacco, lumber, and fish found important markets in Europe and the West Indies. The growth of a generation of people who were born in the colonies and the rise of a new wealthy merchant class began to slowly transform the political and cultural landscape of colonial New England, whose governance continued to be dominated by relatively conservative Puritan leaders.

Cape Ann
As early as 1623, the Plymouth Council for New England had established a small fishing village at Cape Ann under supervision of the new Dorchester Company. The latter had been organized through the efforts of the Puritan minister John White of Dorchester, who has been called "the father of

Massachusetts Bay Colony

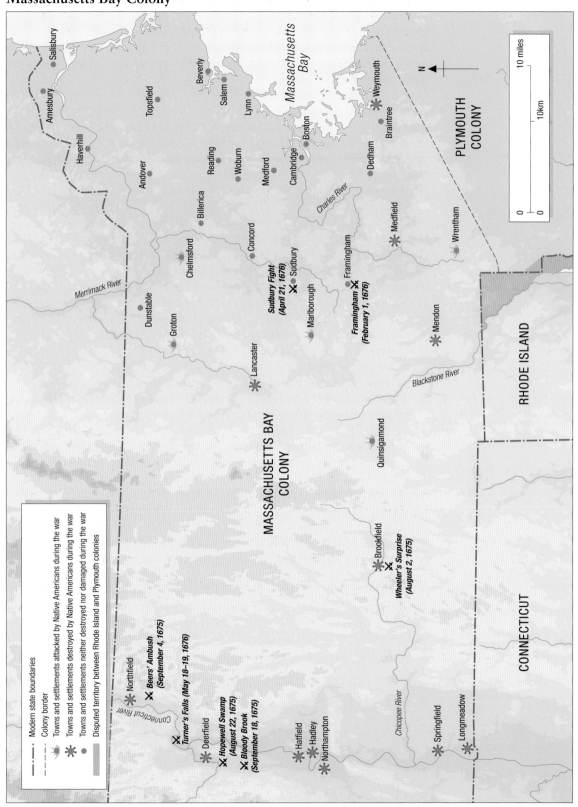

Massachusetts Bay

PLYMOUTH COLONY

RHODE ISLAND

CONNECTICUT

MASSACHUSETTS BAY COLONY

10 miles

10km

N

Salisbury

Amesbury

Haverhill

Topsfield

Beverly

Salem

Lynn

Andover

Reading

Woburn

Medford

Cambridge

Boston

Weymouth

Braintree

Dedham

Billerica

Chelmsford

Concord

Medfield

Wrentham

Merrimack River

Charles River

Dunstable

Groton

Lancaster

Sudbury

Sudbury Fight
(April 21, 1676)

Marlborough

Framingham

Framingham
(February 1, 1676)

Mendon

Blackstone River

Quinsigamond

Brookfield

Wheeler's Surprise
(August 2, 1675)

Northfield

Beers' Ambush
(September 4, 1675)

Turner's Falls (May 18–19, 1676)

Connecticut River

Deerfield

Hopewell Swamp
(August 22, 1675)

Bloody Brook
(September 18, 1675)

Hatfield

Hadley

Northampton

Chicopee River

Springfield

Longmeadow

- - - Modern state boundaries
- – - Colony border
Towns and settlements attacked by Native Americans during the war
Towns and settlements destroyed by Native Americans during the war
Towns and settlements neither destroyed nor damaged during the war
Disputed territory between Rhode Island and Plymouth colonies

Massachusetts Colony." The Cape Ann settlement, however, soon proved unprofitable, and by the end of 1625, the Dorchester Company's financial backers terminated their support for the project. Some of the settlers from Cape Ann, however, decided to remain in New England, and established a new colony further south, near the native village of Naumkeag, under the guidance of Roger Conant.

Massachusetts Bay

Meanwhile, White continued to seek funding to establish a new colony. As a result, the Plymouth Council for New England issued a land grant to a new group of investors that included a few holdovers from the Dorchester Company. The land grant was for territory between the Charles and Merrimack rivers, and the new company was called "The New England Company for a Plantation in Massachusetts Bay." In 1628, the latter sent 100 settlers to join Conant at Naumkeag, the name of which was changed to Salem at some point during the following year. The Massachusetts Bay Colony became the first English chartered colony with governors who did not reside in England; this independence helped the Puritan colonists to perform their religious practices with very little influence from the king and the Anglican Church. It is not clear if King Charles I knew that the company was meant to support Puritan emigration; probably, he assumed that it was formed for business purposes only, as was the custom of the time.

New Hampshire

In the New Hampshire area, the first settlements dated back to 1623 and were mostly inhabited by fishermen who lived near the Piscataqua River. In addition, some plantations protected by small forts were built in the area during the early 1630s. From the outset, the New Hampshire colonists had to endure hostility from the indigenous locals, and as a result, in 1631 a professional soldier was dispatched to the new settlements to organize a

A colonial house from the time of King Philip's War: Deane Winthrop House in Winthrop, MA. Built in 1675 and partly modified in 1696, its owner was Deane Winthrop, sixth son of John Winthrop the Elder, who was Governor of Massachusetts Bay Colony several times between 1630 and 1649. (CC BY-SA 3.0, Wikimedia Commons/Jameslwoodward)

militia and train the local colonists in martial skills. In 1641, the settlements of the Piscataqua River area passed under the jurisdiction of Massachusetts, and their men became part of the Massachusetts Militia. New Hampshire Colony would once again become independent in 1679, when it was separated from Massachusetts by royal order.

Maine

To the north of New Hampshire lay Maine, which also formed part of Massachusetts Bay Colony. Once again, the colonists who settled here were exposed to Native American attacks, notably following the outbreak of informal hostilities with French colonists in Canada. The latter led to raids being carried out on the northern borders of New England.

Saybrook and New Haven colonies

Saybrook Colony was established in late 1635 at the mouth of the Connecticut River by John Winthrop the Younger, who was the son of the Governor of the Massachusetts Bay Colony, John Winthrop the Elder. By 1638, however, funding difficulties meant that plans for expanding Saybrook had to be abandoned. As a consequence, the existing colony struggled, and in 1644 it was merged with Connecticut Colony lying a few miles upriver.

In 1665, Connecticut Colony also incorporated the territory of New Haven Colony, which had been founded by Puritan settlers in 1637. New Haven had never had a charter granting it a legal title to exist, and it fell under the shadow of the larger neighboring colony of Connecticut to the north. Its founders were never able to build up a sufficiently profitable trading base, as it lay on poor agricultural land, and was relatively isolated. Its towns gradually came under Connecticut's sway between 1662 and 1664.

Connecticut

During the early months of 1636, a group of 250 colonists from Massachusetts, led by Thomas Hooker, settled on the west bank of the Connecticut River. One of the reasons why Hooker had decided to leave Massachusetts Bay Colony was that only members of the Puritan Church could vote and participate in the government of the colony. Instead, Hooker believed that any adult male owning property should have had the right to vote and take part in the political life of the colony.

Although the Connecticut colonists did not initially organize any militia, relations with the local Pequot Native Americans (the most important tribe in the area) became increasingly tense. In the early 1630s, the Connecticut River Valley was in a state of turmoil: the Pequots were aggressively expanding their area at the expense of neighbouring tribes, including the Wampanoags and Narragansetts, and the Mohegans, who had separated from them. All these tribes contended for political dominance and control over the fur trade with the Europeans. The colonists were gradually extending their control over trading in fur and wampum (the Narragansetts and Pequots had controlled the latter up until 1633). As a result, a series of incidents and minor skirmishes took place between settler and native, increasing tensions on both sides.

In one notable incident, John Stone, an English smuggler and privateer, was murdered with seven of his crew by the Niantics, a western tributary group of the Pequots. Following Stone's death, the leaders of Massachusetts

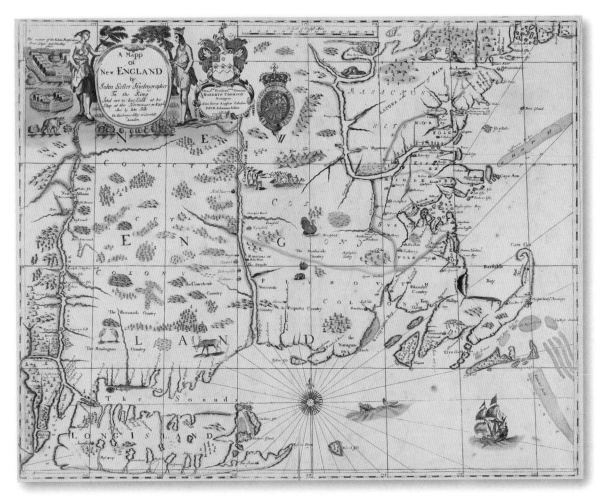

John Seller's *Mapp of New England*, published in 1675. The conflict in the Connecticut River Valley is clearly shown. (Public domain)

Bay Colony protested to the Pequots. The latter answered that Stone's death had been an accident: the Niantics had attacked him thinking that he and his men were Dutch, not English. The Pequots sent wampum to atone for the killing, but refused the colonial authorities' demand that the warriors responsible for Stone's death be turned over for trial and punishment.

On July 20, 1636, a respected trader named John Oldham was attacked while on a voyage to Block Island. He and several of his crew were killed, and his ship was looted by allies of the Narragansetts, who sought to discourage settlers from trading with their Pequot rivals. In August, Henry Vane, the governor of Massachusetts Bay Colony, sent a party of 90 militiamen led by John Endecott to exact revenge on the natives of Block Island. Endecott's men attacked two Niantic villages and burned them to the ground. Endecott then went on to attack other native settlements.

The Pequots were outraged by Endecott's actions, and attempted to form a tribal alliance, with limited success. The Pequots' traditional enemies, the Mohegans and Narragansetts, openly sided with the colonists. The Narragansetts had lost significant territory to the Pequots in 1622, and were thus easily convinced to side with the settlers and fight the Pequots.

During the autumn and winter of 1636/37, Saybrook Colony was practically under siege: those who ventured outside the fort were killed by the Pequots. With the arrival of spring, the Native Americans increased the

Plymouth Colony and Rhode Island Colony

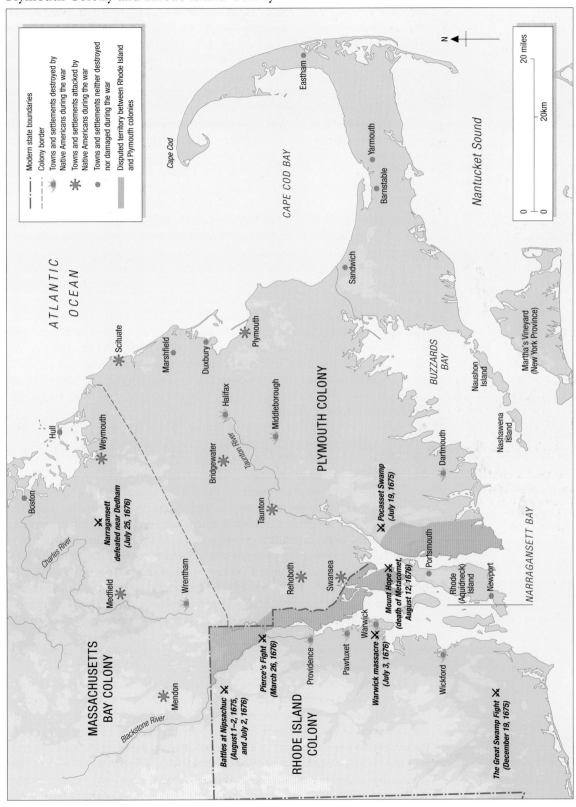

Legend:
- Modern state boundaries
- Colony border
- Towns and settlements destroyed by Native Americans during the war
- Towns and settlements attacked by Native Americans during the war
- Towns and settlements neither destroyed nor damaged during the war
- Disputed territory between Rhode Island and Plymouth colonies

N

20 miles
20km

ATLANTIC OCEAN

CAPE COD BAY

Cape Cod

Eastham

Yarmouth
Barnstable

Sandwich

Nantucket Sound

Scituate

Marshfield
Duxbury

Plymouth

Halifax

Middleborough

Taunton River

PLYMOUTH COLONY

BUZZARDS BAY

Dartmouth

Nashawena Island

Naushon Island

Martha's Vineyard (New York Province)

Hull
Weymouth

Bridgewater

Taunton

Pocasset Swamp (July 19, 1675)

Boston

Narragansett defeated near Dedham (July 25, 1676)

Charles River

Wrentham

Rehoboth

Swansea

Mount Hope (death of Metacomet, August 12, 1676)

Portsmouth

Rhode (Aquidneck) Island

Newport

NARRAGANSETT BAY

Medfield

MASSACHUSETTS BAY COLONY

Mendon

Blackstone River

Pierce's Fight (March 26, 1676)

Providence

Pawtuxet

Warwick

Warwick massacre (July 3, 1676)

Wickford

Battles at Nipsachuc (August 1–2, 1675, and July 2, 1676)

RHODE ISLAND COLONY

The Great Swamp Fight (December 19, 1675)

15

number of raids and began to attack the Connecticut colonists. In May, the leaders of the Connecticut River towns met in Hartford and decided to organize a force of militiamen to oppose the attacks. Captain John Mason was put in command of this force, which comprised 90 militiamen and 70 Mohegans. At Fort Saybrook, the militiamen were joined by John Underhill with another 20 men. The expedition sailed to Narragansett Bay, where it gained further support from 200 Narragansett warriors. The force, now totaling 380 men, marched for approximately 20 miles toward Mystic Fort, with the intention of mounting a surprise attack against the Pequots just before dawn. The events of the following day, May 26, 1637, later became known as the Mystic Massacre. The militiamen and their Native American allies surrounded one of the two fortified Pequot villages at Mystic and then used fire to create chaos. The ensuing conflagration trapped the majority of the Pequots inside the village and many died. Those who managed to escape were killed by the militiamen surrounding the village. The savagery of the assault did, however, provoke tensions between the colonists and their Narragansett and Mohegan allies.

In mid-June of the same year, 160 militiamen and 40 allied Native American warriors left Saybrook with the objective of intercepting the Pequot refugees on their way to Mohawk territory. The colonists caught up with the Pequots at Saska, and captured or killed the majority of them, in the Fairfield Swamp Fight. This practically ended the Pequot War, which resulted in the almost complete extinction of the proud Pequot tribe. The Pequot War would be the last significant conflict between the Native Americans and the New England colonists until the outbreak of King Philip's War in 1675.

Providence, Rhode Island

In January 1636, Salem minister Roger Williams was banished from Massachusetts because of theological differences with the ruling leadership of the colony. He preached that government and religion should be separated, and believed that the Wampanoag and Narragansett Native Americans had been poorly and unjustly treated by the New England settlers. After being exiled from Massachusetts, he was helped by the Narragansetts, who sold him land so that he could establish a new colony in present-day Providence (Rhode Island). Williams and his group of colonists settled at the tip of Narragansett Bay, and the new site was called Providence Plantation.

Providence soon became a place of religious freedom, but internal divisions among the colonists led to the formation of two new independent settlements: Portsmouth and Newport. In 1644, however, Providence, Portsmouth, and Newport were integrated to form the new Colony of Rhode Island and Providence Plantations.

EPIDEMICS

The immigrants to New England arrived in a land under attack by invisible enemies, whose weapons were deadlier than any settler's musket or Pequot's tomahawk. For millennia, epidemics of infectious diseases had ravaged the heavily populated areas of Europe and Asia. Outbreaks of typhus and diphtheria, smallpox and measles, the bubonic plague, and other diseases had sometimes killed tens of millions. It was worst in the cities. London, for

The visitors and colonists from the Old World brought with them diseases against which the Indians had no immunity. These included smallpox, tuberculosis, cholera, and measles. Successive outbreaks had devastating impacts on the Native American populations in the 17th century. (Public domain)

example, had an epidemic of smallpox in 1602, and epidemics of the plague in 1603 and 1606. In 1625, the plague returned, killing 35,000, and again in 1665, killing 100,000.

There was no safety in New England. Four years before the arrival of the Pilgrims at Plymouth, smallpox had ravaged the Native American nations in New England, killing about 75 percent of those affected. As the immigrants arrived, smallpox returned between 1628 and 1631, and again in 1633. Typhus came in 1638. Smallpox returned between 1648 and 1649. Measles came in 1657 and 1658, and diphtheria in 1659.

The diseases killed settler and Native American alike, but the effect on the populations was very different. The infected settlers were much more likely to survive. An outbreak that killed eight or nine out of every 10 infected Native Americans might kill only one or two out of 10 infected settlers.

Neither the Puritans, who attributed the afflictions to the will of God, nor the Native Americans, who believed that inexplicable deaths were the work of evil spirits or witches, understood the causes of the epidemics, but their effect was obvious to both. The English population, swollen by new immigrants every year, increased. The Native American population decreased. By 1675, the settlers greatly outnumbered the Native Americans.

MILITARY COOPERATION BETWEEN THE COLONIES

At the conclusion of the English Civil Wars, the settlers of Massachusetts Bay Colony faced several political problems. As previously noted, the Puritan colonists of Massachusetts supported both the English Commonwealth and the Protectorate of Cromwell, which naturally presented problems on

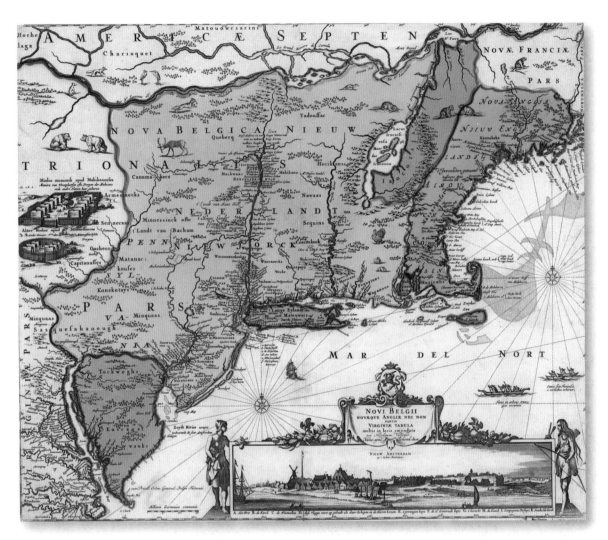

A map by Nicolaes Visscher of north-eastern America, showing New England (Nova Anglia, red) and New Netherland (Nova Belgica, yellow), originally published in Amsterdam in 1656. Green areas indicate those still under Native American control. The jurisdiction of Long Island (Lange Eylandt) was originally split between the Dutch and English, until 1664, when the English took over New Netherland, including Long Island. (Library of Congress; public domain)

the restoration of the monarchy in 1660. King Charles II sought to extend royal influence over New England, something that Massachusetts resisted with more determination than any other colony. The settlers repeatedly refused requests by Charles and his agents to allow the Church of England to become established on Massachusetts territory; in addition, they resisted adherence to any new law that could constrain colonial trade. For the Puritan colonists, the king had no authority to control the governance of the North American settlements.

In order to resist the pressure coming from England, and to defend against possible attacks by the Dutch or Native Americans, Massachusetts concluded a formal military alliance with Plymouth and the other New England colonies in 1634. As the New England Confederation, they would attempt to coordinate their militia forces for their common defense. The Puritans made no effort to include the other English colonies, Virginia and Maryland, which had been founded in 1632 by a group of Catholic refugees under a charter obtained by George Calvert from King Charles I. The New England Confederation, however, collapsed in 1654 when Massachusetts refused to join an expedition against New Netherland during the First Anglo-Dutch War.

By 1675, the number of English colonies in North America had grown to eight. The New England colonies had been consolidated into four: Plymouth, Massachusetts, Rhode Island, and Connecticut. King Philip's War would force them to create a new alliance.

Beyond New England, Virginia and Maryland had been joined by two more colonies. To the west was New York, which had been Dutch New Netherland. Taken and renamed by the English in 1664, it had been reconquered by the Dutch in 1673, and then permanently surrendered to the English in 1674 at the end of the Third Anglo-Dutch War. Far to the south was Carolina, founded in 1670 at Charleston, SC. Those colonies, however, would play no part in King Philip's War.

RISING TENSIONS

Peace provided many advantages to both the colonists and Native Americans. The colonists could provide a variety of goods manufactured in England, especially metal weapons and tools, which were far superior to the stone equivalents that the Native Americans could make for themselves. The Native Americans could provide allies in time of war, instruction in better methods for living in the New England woods, furs and hides, and a source of hired labor. In the relatively small area of New England, mutual attraction brought the colonists and Native Americans into closer and more frequent proximity than was common in the other English colonies.

Such proximity, however, increased the effect of misunderstandings and cultural incompatibilities between the groups. Elsewhere, those were minimized. In Virginia, for example, a boundary line divided the areas in which the colonists and Native Americans lived, and crossing it without permission subjected both colonists and Native Americans to severe penalties. The cultural differences in New England, moreover, were especially stark because the colonists were Puritans.

In all things, the Puritans saw at work the hand of God. Among the reasons they had been sent to New England, the Puritan leaders agreed, was to be the bridge by which the Native Americans destined for salvation could become Puritans. They devoted considerable resources to that end. Soon after the founding of Harvard College, arrangements were made for Native American converts, like the Massachusett John Sassamon, to obtain there the learning needed to become ministers to their peoples. A Puritan scholar, aided by Sassamon and three Massachuset translators, then undertook a laborious and expensive task. In 1663, there appeared from a printing press imported from England 1,000 copies of a 1,081-page work: the entire Bible translated into Massachusett language.

By 1675, almost all the Massachusetts, and many other New England Native Americans, mostly women and children, had become Christians. About a fifth of the Native Americans were what the colonists called "Praying Indians." Those who had not converted were not persecuted. Even the Native American shamans, whom the Puritans considered active agents of Satan, were allowed to continue their investigations in the spirit world. But the laws of the Puritan colonies and particular towns banned the practice of heathen rites in public, where they might be seen by the faithful.

A map of New England, from Hubbard's *A Narrative of the Troubles with the Indians in New-England* (1677). North points to the right-hand side of the map.

Many other practices that were customary among the Native Americans, such as traveling on the Sabbath, and dressing in immodest clothing, also were banned. Offenders usually were fined. Those who could not pay, like most Native Americans, were sentenced to periods of labor to repay their debts. Such sentences humiliated Native American men, especially when they were sentenced to farm labor. They considered such work as proper for women, children, and slaves, and degrading for men who were hunters and warriors.

The proximity also created conflicts over the use of land. Native American nations claimed vast areas, usually bounded by streams. They used specific locations for towns, hunting camps, fields of crops, religious or burial sites, large patches of edible berries, or sources of a usable mineral, and the whole area for movement and hunting. Nations might war if use of a specific location was contested, and sometimes to stop other nations from using their land for movement or hunting. An individual, however, seldom had reason to think that someone was denying him his personal rights.

Most of the settlers, however, had personal rights to land purchased from an Indian nation. Each New England colony enacted its own legislation regulating such purchases: Massachusetts in 1634, Maryland in 1639, Plymouth in 1643, Rhode Island in 1651, and Connecticut in 1663. By 1675, the purchases had created a serious problem. New England had become a rough patchwork of large areas used by the Indians for their purposes, and smaller, privately owned parcels of land.

The settlers claimed personal rights arising from English law and that of their colony. English land law was very complicated, but also very flexible. It defined land on paper, as large or small areas with boundaries described so that a court could resolve a dispute over where they ran. It allowed multiple persons to acquire different rights to the use of the same land, either permanently or for a period of time. It allowed individuals to succeed to the rights of others by sale or gift, inheritance or contract, or to obtain rights for themselves by uncontested use.

English law also allowed individuals to obtain papers giving them an exclusive right to use an area of land in any way, to exclude all others as trespassers, and to transfer the land to someone else. Those who had such a right generally called themselves "owners" of land. The settlers who purchased land from the Native Americans used as models papers by which persons became owners.

The Native Americans, who relied upon hunting as a source of food, usually did not know where the boundaries of a settler's land even were. They assumed that, as long as they avoided settlers' houses, farm structures, and fields, they were offending no one. Nonetheless, if they were found within the boundaries of a settler's land, they might be charged as trespassers and fined. To the Native Americans, such action seemed petty and hostile. Every year, more settlers became owners of land. As ever more land was closed to them, the anger of the frustrated Native American hunters grew.

THE RISE OF METACOMET

The Wampanoags were among the first native communities to have contact with the colonists, as English merchant vessels and fishing boats explored the coast of New England in the early 17th century. When the first English settlers disembarked on Wampanoag land, the sachem was Massasoit, father to the yet-to-be-born Metacomet. Massasoit, seeing that the newcomers were few in number but heavily armed, decided to adopt a friendly posture from the outset.

At this time, Massasoit was seeking to affirm his dominance as the regional sachem. He understood that he could use the colonists as powerful allies in his conflicts against bordering tribes. The Wampanoags then taught the settlers how to cultivate the "Three Sisters" (i.e. the three main agricultural crops of New England) —corn, squash, and beans. They also showed them how to catch and process fish, which could be found in abundance along the coast. In 1621, Massasoit's Wampanoags and the early Plymouth colonists joined to celebrate their friendship on a famous occasion. It would be remembered as the first Thanksgiving, and in time become an American national holiday.

In 1632, the Wampanoags came under attack by the powerful Narragansett tribe. The Wampanoags and Narragansetts had always been strong regional rivals, but the arrival of the colonists had worsened relations between the two tribes. The colonists soon came to the aid of their Wampanoag allies, and their help was decisive in repulsing the Narragansetts. Massasoit's status as sachem was increasingly dependent on the support of his colonist allies.

In 1643, the Mohegans defeated the Narragansetts, and the latter began a general movement of population toward Wampanoag territory. This time, however, the two tribes did not clash, but began to cooperate. By 1650, a good number of Wampanoags, especially women, had been converted to Christianity, and Massasoit himself had begun to adopt a colonist lifestyle. During the closing phase of his life, the sachem even asked the legislators of Plymouth Colony to bestow English names on both of his sons. The eldest, Wamsutta, was given the name Alexander; Metacomet was given the name Philip.

PHILIP. *KING* of Mount Hope.

P.Revere *sc*

The best-known portrait of King Philip, from the 1772 edition of Benjamin Church's memoirs *The Entertaining History of King Philip's War*. Later depictions of Metacomet were heavily influenced by this portrait. King Philip is shown holding a musket, while in the background Native Americans prepare for war. This portrait by Paul Revere was probably based on an engraved portrait of Ho Nee Yeath Tan No Row, an Iroquois chief who traveled to Great Britain to meet Queen Anne in 1710. (Public domain)

Wamsutta shared the strategic vision of his sachem father, and wished to continue good relations with the colonists. Metacomet, in contrast, had a completely different point of view, and felt strongly that the settlers had no right to stay and live on the land that had always belonged to the Wampanoag tribe.

In 1661, when Metacomet was 23 years old, sachem Massasoit died. Wamsutta, as expected, became chief of the Wampanoags. Shortly afterwards, Wamsutta was forced by the colonial authorities to go to Marshfield so that he could be interrogated by the Governor of Plymouth. The colonists were concerned about the new chief's intentions, and feared that he could rise up in revolt against them. The meeting between the native leader and the colonial authorities ended positively, but while returning to his village, Wamsutta became seriously ill and died shortly after. The Wampanoag chief probably died of fever, but many Wampanoags thought that he had been poisoned by the colonists during his stay.

In 1662, within a year of Massasoit's death, Metacomet became chief of the Wampanoag tribe and assumed the role of sachem. Under his new leadership, the previous disposition of the Wampanoags toward the colonists changed dramatically. Metacomet, who had been raised to be a model woodland warrior from his early years, strongly believed that with the progression of time, the settlers would eventually take everything away from the Native Americans of New England—not only their lands, but also their culture and traditional way of life. The only way to stop this process was to forge a wider coalition of tribes, which would be strong enough to conduct total war against the settlers, and expel them entirely from New England.

THE PATH TO WAR

In 1667, five years after Metacomet's rise to the leadership of his tribe, rumours about the Wampanoag sachem started to circulate among the English settlers. According to these, King Philip was attempting to form an anti-English military alliance with the French and Dutch, who were at war with England in the Second Anglo-Dutch War. It remains unclear whether the sachem held secret talks with the French or Dutch. In any case, the Second Anglo-Dutch War ended in 1667, and King Philip was able to protest his innocence before the New England colonial authorities. The latter, however, remained convinced that Metacomet was planning something dangerous. While they knew the Wampanoags were not yet ready to wage war, they feared that changes were afoot in the status quo of settler–native relations in New England.

In April 1671, the New England colonial authorities arranged a meeting with Metacomet to better understand his intentions; the colonists of Plymouth had been informed that both the Wampanoags and the Narragansetts appeared to be preparing for war, and they thus wanted to obtain a clearer picture of the situation. King Philip agreed to attend the meeting, which took place at Taunton, MA, albeit without great enthusiasm. At this meeting, the representatives of Plymouth and Massachusetts Bay colonies accused the sachem of preparing to attack their settlements, and requested him to give up all firearms in the possession of the Wampanoags. At that particular moment, King Philip had insufficient men and materiel to commence hostilities against the colonists, and thus agreed to sign a document, known as the Taunton Agreement, consenting to the colonists' requests. In September of the same year, a further agreement was concluded, whose terms stipulated that a fine would be imposed on the Wampanoags, instead of giving up their muskets.

In the wake of these events, tension between the two parties began to escalate rapidly. By accepting the colonists' terms, Metacomet had lost face as sachem, while the settlers had failed to remove the threat posed by firearms in the possession of potentially hostile Native Americans. The four years between 1671 and 1675 were ones of undeclared war: Metacomet completed his lengthy preparations and strengthened his alliances with other tribes, while concern continued to grow among the colonists about Wampanoag intentions.

The casus belli: John Sassamon's death

The most important figures in avoiding war were men like John Sassamon. Fluent in both Native American and English, able to understand the reasoning of both unhappy chiefs like Metacomet and suspicious colonial leaders, and widely respected by both Native Americans and colonists, they were indispensable. Through their voices the Native Americans and colonists could speak to one another, and by their ears each could hear the other. They also were investigators, reporting to each on the plans and actions of the other, and advisors who could offer to each informed counsel on how to respond.

When, however, either the Native Americans or colonists had secrets to be concealed from the other, such men might easily be accused of being spies. In early January 1675, Sassamon reported to the governor of Plymouth Colony that Metacomet's Wampanoags planned to attack the settlements the following summer. On January 29, his body was found. Marks on it indicated that he had been strangled.

A Christian Wampanoag then told the colonists that he had seen three Wampanoag friends of Metacomet kill Sassamon. The three were arrested and tried by a jury composed of both Native Americans and colonists. Although the three protested their innocence, their accuser was believed. They were then executed. As he waited to be hanged, one admitted that the three were guilty. The men's execution on June 8, 1675, was the spark that ignited the flames of King Philip's War.

CHRONOLOGY

1675

June 20
The town of Swansea is attacked by Wampanoags, and several of its houses are looted and destroyed, in the opening action of King Philip's War.

June 21–22
The colonists seek to negotiate with several key tribes, including the Nipmucs and the Narragansetts.

June 27
Taunton is attacked by Native Americans.

June 30
Old Rehoboth is attacked by Native Americans.

June 30–July 1
Colonial military forces under the command of Major Thomas Savage move into Pokanoket Peninsula in search of Metacomet. King Philip's forces escape across Mount Hope Bay, and are joined by other warriors.

July 9
Middleborough and Dartmouth, Massachusetts, are destroyed by Native American warriors.

July 14
The Nipmucs launch an attack against Mendon, Massachusetts Bay Colony.

July 28
Captain Edward Hutchinson meets with Nipmuc chiefs, and apparently secures the neutrality of the tribe.

July 29
King Philip's warriors cross the Taunton River, in the process leaving their families behind. The latter are captured by colonist militiamen and are later sold into slavery.

August 1
The Battle of Nipsachuc, between Metacomet's forces and Mohegan warriors, who are allies of the colonists. King Philip manages to escape capture.

August 2
Wheeler's Surprise: on a diplomatic mission, Captain Hutchinson's party is ambushed and wiped out by Nipmuc warriors led by Muttawmp.

August 2–3
Siege of Brookfield: Muttawmp fails to destroy the only fortified house of the settlement.

August 5
King Philip arrives at Menameset, and joins forces with his allies.

August 22
Lancaster is attacked by Native Americans.

August 25
Battle of Hopewell Swamp; the Norwottucks ambush a colonist militia force, but fail to destroy it.

September 1	Deerfield and Hadley are attacked by Native Americans.
September 4	Having evacuated the settlement of Northfield, Captain Richard Beers and his militiamen are ambushed by Native American warriors.
September 18	Battle of Bloody Brook: Captain Thomas Lathrop and his militiamen are ambushed by Muttawmp while coming to the aid of Deerfield's residents.
October 5	Native Americans attack Springfield during the absence of the local militiamen, who have left the city on an expedition. Most of the settlement is destroyed.
October 19	A Native American assault on Hatfield is repulsed—the first success for the colonists in King Philip's War.
December 19	The Great Swamp Fight: in the largest battle of the war, an army of 1,150 colonists destroys a massive Narragansett fortified camp.

1676

February 10	Lancaster is attacked by Native Americans. Mary Rowlandson is taken captive.
February 21	Medfield is attacked by Native Americans; half of the settlement is destroyed.
March 14	Northampton is attacked, but the Native American assault is repulsed by the defending militiamen.
March 26	Marlborough is attacked by Native Americans; most of the settlement's buildings are destroyed. Pierce's Fight: a force of militiamen moving against the Narragansetts in Rhode Island is wiped out by Native Americans.
March 29	Canonchet's Narragansett warriors destroy Providence, Rhode Island.
April 21	The Sudbury Fight: a large war party led by King Philip attacks Sudbury, and ambushes a force of militiamen coming to the aid of the besieged settlement.
May 19	Battle of Turner's Falls; a colonist militia force destroys a large Native American camp, but is then defeated by an enemy counterattack.
June 12	A Native American attack on Hadley is fought off by the local garrison.
August 12	Metacomet is intercepted by Benjamin Church's rangers at Mount Hope, and is shot dead by John Alderman.

OPPOSING COMMANDERS

NATIVE AMERICAN

Metacomet, also known as Metacom and King Philip, was born in 1638, the second son of Massasoit. As sachem of the Wampanoags in 1675, Metacomet led the Wampanoag warriors and others who joined in his operations. Although he had no power to issue orders to the leaders of other nations' warriors, he was an inspirational figure, and given great respect in the councils in which combined or coordinated operations were planned.

The most important of the other commanders led the Nipmucs and Narragansetts. **Muttawmp** and **Monoco** commanded the Nipmucs. Muttawmp had converted to Christianity, but was one of the first leaders to join Metacomet in his attacks on the settlements. He commanded the Nipmuc and other warriors at Wheeler's Surprise, the Siege of Brookfield, the Battle of Bloody Brook, the Hatfield Raid, and the Sudbury Fight. Monoco, chief of the Nashaway nation of the Nipmucs, led warriors at the Lancaster Raid, the attack on Medfield, and the attack on Groton. **Canonchet**, the last of the commanders to join Metacomet, led the Narragansetts at the Great Swamp Fight, Pierce's Fight, and the destruction of Providence. Like Metacomet, Muttawmp, and Monoco, he ultimately was captured and executed by the colonists.

COLONIST

The two New England colonies that were most heavily involved in King Philip's War were Plymouth and Massachusetts Bay. In 1675, they were ruled respectively by governors Josiah Winslow and John Leverett.

Josiah Winslow was elected Assistant Governor of Plymouth Colony in 1657, and the following year he became Major-Commandant of the colony's militia. On June 3, 1673, he was chosen as the colony's governor. An experienced military leader, Winslow consistently sought to improve the fighting capabilities of his colony: in 1658, he promoted the consolidation of its separate militia companies into a single regiment; and in 1674, he organized a guard corps with four halberdiers, who were to act as bodyguards for the governor and other magistrates of the colony. In contrast to his predecessors, Josiah Winslow did not consider the Native Americans as peaceful trading partners; this attitude, which was shared by Plymouth's colonial government, was clearly evident in the state of readiness maintained in Plymouth after Winslow's election as governor. Conversely, the Native Americans had a low opinion of Winslow, who was considered by many to have been behind Wamsutta's sudden death. Like many second-generation colonists, Winslow's ambition was to acquire new land from the Native Americans as rapidly as, and by any means, possible.

When war broke out in 1675, Governor Winslow was ill with what appears to have been tuberculosis, and thus was unable to take command of the militia. After several colonial defeats in the early phase of the conflict, Winslow understood that the European tactics employed by his militiamen were not well suited to the woodlands of North America, and thus accepted the proposal put forward by Benjamin Church to create a special company of rangers. This choice proved decisive for the outcome of the war—it was one of Church's men who killed Metacomet in 1676.

John Leverett arrived in New England in 1633, and settled with his family in Boston. Six years later, he joined the Artillery Company of Massachusetts,

A 19th-century engraving of Josiah Winslow, after the portrait from life that hangs in the Pilgrim Hall Museum, Plymouth, MA. (*Appletons' Cyclopædia of American Biography*, volume 6, 1888; public domain)

the oldest military organization in North America. In 1644, he returned to England in order to take part in the Civil War, in which he supported the Parliamentary cause. Leverett served as a cavalry commander, and fought with great distinction. After returning to New England, he became a cavalry officer in the Massachusetts militia, and his popularity began to grow. In 1654, Leverett was chosen as Governor of Acadia (present-day Nova Scotia, Canada) and retained this position for three years. Between 1663 and 1673, he was Major-General of the Massachusetts Militia, before being elected governor two years before the outbreak of King Philip's War. During the latter conflict, Leverett made good use of his past experience, and proved to be a skilled and determined leader.

Connecticut Colony was also embroiled in King Philip's War, albeit to a lesser extent than Plymouth and Massachusetts Bay. In 1675, its governor was **John Winthrop the Younger** (1606–76), who had spent most of his early years between New England and Old England. In 1649, he finally decided to settle in New England, and two years later, he received his first major public appointment. After becoming governor of Connecticut in 1659, he spent most of the following years opposing native incursions and consolidating the settlements of his colony. During King Philip's War, having realized that the conflict would shape the futures of all the New England colonies, Winthorp sent his best militiamen against the Native American warriors in support of the governors of Plymouth and Massachusetts. He is remembered to this day as an important man of science, and as one of Connecticut's most important governors.

The most notable and important colonial military commander during King Philip's War was the great tactician **Benjamin Church**, the founding father of the rangers. Church was born in Plymouth Colony in 1639, and was brought up according to colonial practices of the time. During his early years, he learned much about native warfare, and acquired a great knowledge of the

OPPOSITE
A modern reconstruction of Metacomet's appearance. There are no known true likenesses of the sachem, but items such as the club, bowl, and sash have been associated with him. Summer wear for New England Native Americans would consist of light clothing, while in winter, bearskin robes were worn. By the time of King Philip's War, European trade goods, clothes, and blankets were common items in use. (Illustration by Jonathan Smith, copyright Osprey Publishing Ltd.)

woodland terrain that surrounded most of Plymouth Colony. Church was a skilled marksman, but also a great innovator: he was among the first to understand that the only effective way of countering Native American hit-and-run tactics was to emulate them. Until 1675, the various colonial militias had been trained in line with contemporary English practice, which took no account of the broken terrain in which they usually fought. Close formations significantly limited the mobility of the militiamen, and they moved far more slowly than their Native American opponents. When marching in close order, the militiamen could be easily attacked by Native American warriors, who were masters of the ambush. When the Native Americans retreated after briefly engaging their enemy, the militiamen were too slow in their pursuit through the densely forested terrain of New England. With these aspects in mind, and combined with his previous experience, Benjamin Church created a highly mobile corps from select militiamen, who would fight exactly like their Native American opponents. Church's innovative ideas were particularly appreciated by Governor Winslow, who appointed him as his military advisor soon after the outbreak of King Philip's War.

An engraving by Amos Doolittle of John Winthrop the Younger, from *A Complete History of Connecticut* (1797). (Public domain)

A portrait of Benjamin Church (1639–1718), whose rangers played a crucial role during King Philip's War. Note the powder horn he is wearing. The portrait appears in *The Entertaining History of King Philip's War,* and the engraving is by Paul Revere. Post 1676, Church remained one of New England's most important militia commanders and continued to lead his rangers until the end of Queen Anne's War (1702–13)—a conflict related to the War of the Spanish Succession. (Courtesy of the John Carter Brown Library, CC BY-SA 4.0)

Col. *BENJAMIN. CHURCH.*

OPPOSING FORCES

NATIVE AMERICAN

The Native American warriors of New England revered war above all else, and dedicated much of their time to honing their fighting skills. This was achieved by practicing activities that had much common with war, like hunting.

Generally speaking, each tribe was guided by a council of the elders that took the most important political decisions. Formed of older, experienced males, these councils were usually opposed to military expeditions directed against the colonist settlements; inter-tribal warfare, in contrast, was generally accepted by the members of the community. Younger warriors were most likely to be opposed to the colonists, and this could sometimes lead to significant internal disagreements within a tribe. Massasoit, who continued to treat the English settlers as friends to the end of his life, and Metacomet, who was eager to fight them as soon as he became sachem, exemplified the conflict among the Wamapanoags.

Leaders like Massasoit, however, had limited power to force their nations' warriors to remain at peace. Individual warriors often conducted raids against other Native American or English settlements, even though their nations had not declared war. During the middle decades of the 17th century, some young warriors began conducting raids against isolated English settlements or homesteads without any approval by their tribal leaders.

Such raids began simply. A warrior chief would send a messenger to all those warriors considered likely to join in an attack; having accepted, they would smoke tobacco in pipes with the messenger. Then, at a later agreed time, the warriors gathered near the chief's house, where a ceremonial meal would be eaten. The war party would then move on its objective, taking with them supplies such as dried corn, maple-sugar, ammunition for their

Detail from John Seller's *Mapp of New England* produced in 1675—the outbreak of King Philip's War. A Native American fortified settlement is shown; note the wooden stockade and long houses. (New York Public Library, public domain)

A modern reconstruction of a traditional Wampanoag dwelling. (CC BY-SA 4.0, Wikimedia Commons/ Thomas Kelly)

muskets, black powder, materials for repairing moccasins, and traditional medicines.

While moving towards a colonist settlement, the war party was led by the pipe-bearer; he was the most noteworthy warrior, and had the honour of carrying the ceremonial pipe. The war chief would move at the back of the group. Larger war parties could include a drummer, and a warrior carrying an eagle-feather banner. The journey to the settlement targeted could last for days, with the warriors making camp en route. A Native American warrior of the 17th century could easily cover 25 miles in a single day, moving much faster than any colonist opponent. One or more of the warriors was tasked with carrying extra ammunition and supplies, in order to provide these for his companions if needed.

Their attacks usually took place at the beginning or at the end of the day, when their movements were more difficult to spot. Having positioned themselves around the colonist settlement and lain in wait, the order was given to launch a surprise attack. Such attacks were mostly conducted to steal goods and supplies of every kind from the colonists, but sometimes prisoners also were taken for use as slaves.

Weaponry

Before the arrival of the Europeans, the Native American warriors of New England employed three main weapons: the bow, the stone tomahawk, and the war club. The latter was a heavy, deadly weapon, made of ironwood or maple, with a large ball or knot at the end. The shaft of each war club was extremely sharp and could inflict terrible wounds when used in close combat. Often, war clubs also had sharp-pointed horns at their shoulders.

Before the arrival of the first settlers, the Native Americans had begun buying from European traders hatchets with blades of iron or steel. Those quickly replaced traditional stone tomahawks. Such trade tomahawks were resistant to damage, and were easy to throw. Some included on the butt opposite the blade a bowl that could be filled with tobacco. The weapon could then also serve as a pipe, smoked through a channel bored through the tomahawk's handle. Steel knives also replaced stone weapons. The advent of trade tomahawks also reduced the popularity of war clubs, which were more difficult to throw.

The early European traders and colonists refused to sell firearms to the Native Americans, who instead used bows and arrows. Native bows were usually of one piece, and made from ash, hickory, or oak. Arrows had triangular chert heads and were carried in cornhusk quivers. In 1637, however, the French began selling matchlock smoothbore muskets to their Native American allies. The Dutch and English followed, and soon began selling flintlocks. Those weapons revolutionized Native American warfare, and replaced the bow and arrow.

Although the Native American warriors of New England never fought on horseback, they otherwise were armed much like their colonial opponents by 1675. With a steel tomahawk or war club, and a steel knife, they were ready for close combat. With flintlock muskets, powder horns and bags full

of musket balls, and often a bow and quiver of arrows as well, they were prepared for battling more distant enemies.

A European flintlock musket mechanism dating from the period 1660–70, remounted on a later 17th-century stock. The flintlock had largely superseded the matchlock musket by the time of King Philip's War. (Livrustkammaren [The Royal Armoury]/Matti Östling/ CC BY-SA 3.0)

COLONIST

In the English colonies of North America, all able-bodied males aged between 16 and 60, be they freemen or servants, were compelled to be listed into their local militia rolls and to attend musters or training days. The latter occasions were usually regarded as important events: particularly in the early years of colonization, the survival of a community and its settlement depended entirely on the efficiency of its militia forces.

The frequency of training varied considerably, according to the period and the location. In the early 17th century, Massachusetts militiamen trained once a week. Later in the century, training occurred on only a few days throughout the year. The frequency and intensity of training tended to increase in more isolated or remote communities, for the obvious reason that they would need to survive on their own for longer. As time progressed, some social categories began to be exempted from service in the militia: magistrates, public notaries, deputies to a legislature, ministers of the church, schoolmasters, students, physicians, masters of ships, fishermen, and herdsmen. All militiamen were required to present themselves at training days properly armed and equipped; in addition, they had to respond to the call of colonial governors in times of emergency. In times of relative peace, the activities of the militia were conducted on a local basis and for limited durations.

In the early colonial period, military commanders usually came from local prominent families, and were chosen by popular vote, as opposed to for their military skills. They had various administrative obligations besides bearing

A display of weapons from King Philip's War (from top to bottom): hatchet, cutlass, early matchlock, late matchlock, early doglock flintlock musket, late doglock flintlock musket, late snaphance flintlock musket, doglock flintlock musket, and early snaphance flintlock musket. The war took place during a transitional period in firearms, with matchlocks being replaced by flintlocks. Hatchets and cutlasses were useful secondary weapons for hand-to-hand fighting. (Photo courtesy of Kenneth Grant)

arms: senior officers, for example, usually had to pay for their company's drums and colors. Officers were unpaid, but serving in the colonial militia had a series of positive effects on the social life of a young officer. Senior officers were usually appointed by the colonial legislature, while junior ones were usually chosen by their men by ballot. As time passed, this situation gradually changed, resulting in the birth of a new and much more professional class of colonial officers.

The early militia units were organized along similar lines to the contemporary English trained bands, with proportions of musketeers and pikemen. Initially, each militia company numbered about 50 men, coming from the same village or town ward; it could be an independent unit or it could be part of a larger county regiment. With regards to cavalry and artillery, troops of mounted militiamen appeared only in the 1640s, while artillerymen were usually individual specialists rather than gunners grouped into single units.

Weaponry

The laws governing the militia contained various specific requirements regarding the weapons and equipment that each militiaman had to carry: those who failed to meet these were usually fined, with the money used to purchase flags and drums for their company. By the mid-17th century, pikes and armor had become rare, and heavy matchlock muskets with rests were gradually being replaced by lighter flintlock snaphance muskets.

Warfare in colonial America, especially in the earlier period, was challenging: the settlers, before facing any Native American threat, had to survive in a challenging and at times hostile natural environment. The first and main objective of every community was that of survival. With only sporadic supply available from overseas, the settlers were obliged to improvise every necessity from the few materials that were locally available.

Shipments coming from Europe arrived in small amounts, at great cost, and took considerable time to reach New England.

Thus, the effort required to maintain a military force under arms was much greater than in Europe. The size of colonial forces was small compared to those of the contemporary European units: minor clashes in European terms would assume far greater importance in New England. Movement across the extensive terrain of New England posed a considerable risk in itself for any military expedition: at times the environment could pose as much of a threat as the Native American warriors hostile to settlement. Close-order, pitched battles were not appropriate to most of the terrain, which ruled out rigid European-style maneuvers and made any use of cavalry practically impossible. Moreover, in the colonies there were too few men available to assemble massed infantry regiments or battalions on a European scale, and we should remember that the independent spirit of most of the colonists usually pitted itself against European ideas of regimentation and deference to authority.

In forested terrain, the Native Americans held the clear tactical advantage: their traditional culture, based on hunting, forged them for a war of silent stalking and ambush. The first European settlers who adapted to employing Native American war methods were fur trappers and hunters, who lived a harsh life in the more remotely settled areas of the colonies. They soon learned how to live in such a challenging, risk-filled environment, becoming as wiley and as ruthless as the Native Americans. When war came, these hunters and trappers were perfectly skilled to act as guides for militiamen from the larger settlements, with their greater experience of movement through the woods, and stealth, than the majority of the settlers. It was from among these men that, in 1675, Benjamin Church recruited his rangers.

A New England militiaman from the period of King Philip's War. Felt hats and simple coats were standard wear. His personal equipment includes a white canvas haversack and a ventral ammunition pouch made of leather. Weaponry comprises a flintlock pistol, a cutlass, and flintlock musket. (Photo courtesy of Kenneth Grant)

Plymouth Colony militia

The first military leader of Plymouth Colony was Myles Standish, an expert soldier who possessed a sound military knowledge, especially in engineering. In 1622, he organized the militia of his community around four infantry companies. Contemporary sources indicate that the militiamen of Plymouth were well trained; Isaack de Rasieres, Secretary of New Netherland Colony, wrote the following description of the militia during a visit to Plymouth Colony in 1627:

> [The] men assemble by beat of the drum, each with his musket or firelock, in front of the captain's door; they have their cloaks on, and place themselves in order, three abreast, and are led by a sergeant without beat of drum. Behind him comes the governor in a long robe; beside him, on the right hand, comes

the preacher with his robe on, and on the left hand the captain with his side-arms, and cloak on, and with a small cane in his hand; and so they march in good order, and each sets his arms down near him. Thus they are constantly on their guard night and day.

Like contemporary militiamen back in England, the early colonist militia used various types of firearms, edged weapons, and armor. Helmets and corselets remained popular until the mid-1630s but then gradually fell out of use. From the mid-17th century, flintlock muskets became more common, replacing older matchlock firearms.

In time, more trained-band companies were formed in the growing number of communities that were established beyond the colony's center. In 1658, all the Plymouth militia infantry companies were consolidated into a single regiment and a troop of horse was added to the existing forces, as well as a senior staff headed by a major.

Church's Rangers

During King Philip's War, Plymouth Colony retained the basic organization of its militia, but a new Company of Volunteers numbering about 200 men was raised in July 1676 for full-time service. This was the famous ranger company created and led by Benjamin Church, which played a crucial role in the war against Metacomet and his allies. Holding the rank of captain, Benjamin Church was given permission to form a company of 200 militiamen, which was to be independent from the Plymouth governor's direct command.

One of Benjamin Church's rangers. Rangers wore a mix of European and Native American items, in contrast to other militiamen. Rangers were particularly adept at traveling long distances on foot and surviving for long periods on little food. (Illustration by Gary Zaboly, copyright Osprey Publishing Ltd.)

Church's company comprised mixed personnel: of the 200 rangers, some 140 were friendly Native Americans who had chosen to serve under Church's command against Metacomet's forces. Benjamin Church was the first colonial officer allowed to recruit Native Americans, using them not only as scouts, but also as fighters. He persuaded many neutral or formerly hostile Native Americans to join his company as irregulars, and some of these even converted to Christianity. With their support, Church's rangers were able to track enemy Native Americans into the dense forests, and ambush them.

Because Church designed his new force primarily to emulate Native American patterns of war, he employed these Native Americans as instructors for the colonist rangers. Under their instruction, Church's militiamen became skilled in fighting in the broken terrain of New England's woodlands. They were trained to organize ambushes, advance steadily in wooded terrain, fire with accuracy, and reload their muskets rapidly. The rangers also learned Native American techniques of hand-to-hand fighting using tomahawks and hatchets. Church's men used their own clothing and weapons, being without uniform; common items of equipment were moccasins and small hatchets, which Church recommended they carry. These woodland warriors were akin to mounted infantry in that they moved rapidly on horseback on flat and open terrain, but dismounted to fight. When moving through broken terrain or woodland, they traveled on foot.

In contrast to other militiamen, who were part-time soldiers that trained for only a few days each year and were called to serve only when needed, the rangers formed a special standing unit. According to Governor Winslow, they were to be employed as raiders, to strike against any hostile tribes using their own tactics. During the early phase of the conflict, King Philip's warriors destroyed numerous colonist settlements with impunity, as they knew that the settlers were in no condition to launch retaliatory actions against their villages. With the creation of Benjamin Church's rangers, all this changed: now, the colonists had a special force that was capable of conducting penetrating raids into enemy territory. In addition, during a Native American raid, the rangers could be employed as fast-moving first responders to counter the threat. During the conflict, Church's rangers proved decisive on several occasions; at the Great Swamp Fight (in which Benjamin Church was wounded) they killed many Native American warriors. The tactical success of the rangers peaked with Metacomet's death, which effectively brought the war to an end.

A living history reenactor poses as one of Benjamin Church's rangers. Simple knit caps made of wool were popular, especially in colder weather. Personal equipment included a wooden flask containing black powder and a canteen made of leather. (Photo courtesy of Kenneth Grant)

Massachusetts Bay Colony

The founding of Massachusetts Bay Colony in 1628 was unopposed by the indigenous Native American tribes; however, from the early beginnings of the settlement, all able-bodied men of Massachusetts were required to bear arms. The first group of Puritan settlers arrived in New England with the following equipment: 80 "bastard snaphance" muskets (with 4ft barrels, but no rests), ten matchlock muskets (4ft barrels, and rests), 60 suits of pikemen's armor (painted in black), 60 pikes, 20 half-pikes, and some halberds or partizans (purchased by the Massachusetts Bay Company). In addition, all the militiamen of the early period were armed with swords; the majority of these were straight and slim-bladed thrusting weapons, but others were broad cutlasses used for delivering slashing cuts. For additional protection, many militiamen employed privately purchased helmets and buff leather coats; by the outbreak of King Philip's War, helmets were no longer in use. Musketeers carried bandoliers with bullet bags and swords; pikemen had helmets, breast and back plates of armor with tassets, pikes, and swords. Usually, in a militia company, there were two musketeers for every pikeman. Captains and lieutenants were armed with partizans, while sergeants had halberds.

Each company had drummers and ensigns who carried the unit's colors. In general terms, as in Plymouth Colony, the English trained bands system was

A colonial militiaman from New Hampshire, armed with a matchlock musket and a cutlass. He holds a Native American war club. He wears a protective buff coat, which might offer some protection against arrows, but not against musket shot. Note the rudimentary canteen carved from a dried-out gourd. (Photo courtesy of Kenneth Grant)

copied closely by the Massachusetts militia. In March 1631, the colonial authorities in Boston ordered that all able-bodied men living in the city should be furnished with good and sufficient weapons for defence of the settlement, which would be provided by the city's government if the individual could not afford them. From July of the same year, two professional military instructors, recruited during the previous year, began to drill the militiamen on the first Friday of every month, to improve their military efficiency.

During the period October to December 1636, the militia companies of Massachusetts Bay Colony were assembled into three regiments: East, North, and South. The East Regiment was the most important one, including militia companies from Boston, Roxburry, Dorchester, Weymouth, and Hingham. Beyond this new organization, there were still several independent companies raised in the smaller outlying communities.

According to a document dating back to 1638, the militiamen serving in the three regiments were to carry the following pieces of equipment: light armor, musket (with a 5ft barrel), sword, bandolier, belt, and ammunition. Around half of the men had to possess armor, but all had to have muskets and swords.

With the general growth in the number of militia units, a need arose for specialized training. As a result, during 1637, proposals were made in Boston to set up a unit to provide training for militia officers and artillery services. The idea was that of creating something similar to the City of London's Artillery Garden, which later became known as the Honourable Artillery Company. On March 13, 1638, the colonial authorities granted a charter for the creation of a Military Company of Massachusetts, whose first commander was the veteran Captain Robert Keayne (who had served in the London Company). Under Keayne's guidance, the new company became the first military training unit and the first artillery school of the American colonies. Many future militia officers underwent their initial training in the ranks of this special institution.

In 1643, the militia was reorganized once again, with the creation of new county regiments that bore the names of their respective counties.

As in the other New England colonies, cavalry in the Massachusetts militia appeared only at a later date; around 1650, when horses were becoming increasingly common in New England, a first troop was formed. Originally, members of this unit were militiamen who acted as mounted soldiers only when their own county regiment was not undergoing exercises. During the following years, more troops of horse were formed; by 1667, there were 12 of them, with 160 cavalrymen in each. Each trooper, like the foot militiaman, was required to furnish arms and equipment for himself (in addition to his horse). The equipment of these mounted militiamen included the following elements: buff coats, pistols, hangers, and corselets. Their superior mobility meant they were put to good use during the colonist operations of King Philip's War.

In 1675, the Massachusetts colonial militia consisted of all males between 16 and 60, who trained eight times per year. Each town also had some artillerymen, who trained every week. By the outbreak of King Philip's War, pikemen had become obsolete. In the summer of 1675, when Metacomet launched his assaults against the colonies of New England, Massachusetts immediately mobilized 700 infantrymen and 200 horsemen in liaison with Plymouth Colony. The foot militiamen were grouped into a provisional Massachusetts Regiment, which took part in several important actions.

Connecticut militia

Around 1660, the colonial militia of Connecticut numbered around 800 men, including a troop of horse raised in Hartford in 1658. Following the Dutch recapture of New Amsterdam in 1673, Connecticut's colonial authorities ordered 500 militiamen to serve as mounted patrols along the coastline. During King Philip's War, in November 1675, Connecticut contributed to the New England colonist war effort by sending a force of 315 militiamen, who were assembled in a single Connecticut Regiment. In addition, 350 militia dragoons were employed against the Native Americans; these men had to provide their own horses, weapons, equipment, and clothing, but would be compensated by the colonial government for any subsequent loss to property during militia service.

The colonists relied on the support of their Native American allies during the war. Uncas, a sachem of the Mohegans, led his forces in joint attacks with the colonists against the Wampanoags and Narragansetts. This image shows Uncas instructing the capture of Miantonomo (father of Canonchet), a Narragansett leader who had invaded Mohegan territory in 1643. (Public domain)

NATIVE AMERICAN ALLIES

The Native American warriors who fought with the colonists made a critical contribution to the forces that opposed King Philip's warriors. They were in three groups. The first group was the Christian Massachusetts, Niantics, and warriors from other nations, generally called the "Praying Indians." Numbering about 200, most fought in Church's Rangers. The second group was the Mohegans, who numbered about 250. Led by their chiefs Uncas and his son Oneko, they defeated Metacomet's Wampanoags at Nipsachuc, and, supporting the colonists, the Narragansetts at the Great Swamp Fight. The third group was the powerful Mohawks. Like a thunderbolt, 900 would appear from nowhere and destroy the Wampanoags in battle in early 1676.

OPPOSING PLANS

NATIVE AMERICAN

Metacomet's plans for the war were relatively simple, but needed lengthy preparation to be put into action. The underlying principle was to launch a series of successive raids against the colonist settlements, attacking smaller, lightly defended ones that were located in remote or isolated areas first. Having destroyed these, the Native American coalition of warriors would launch larger raids against more well-established colonist towns and centers.

The conflict would begin at low intensity and on a small scale, involving just a few hundred Native American warriors; after their initial successes, it would progressively transform into a larger, total war involving most of New England and a wider coalition of tribes. The ultimate objective was to destroy all the colonial settlements of the region, or at least to inflict such severe human and material losses on the colonists that they would be forced to abandon New England altogether.

At the outbreak of the conflict, King Philip had limited military resources at his disposal, given that he could only count on his Wampanoag warriors—a further reason why small-scale attacks were to be preferred in the initial phase of operations. Metacomet understood, however, that any preliminary successes would encourage other tribes in New England to join his cause, thus increasing his resources and manpower, and allowing him to plan more ambitious attacks against larger colonial settlements.

The opening phase of the war would thus be extremely important from a psychological point of view. If the colonists felt sufficient terror of the violence of Metacomet's raids, their will

The Paul Revere House in Boston, MA, was built around 1680 on the site of the former home of Increase Mather (destroyed by fire in 1676). Its robust construction is typical of a colonist stronghouse of the First Period. An estimated 90 percent of the structure is original to 1680. (Wikimedia Commons/ Urban~commonswiki, CC BY-SA 3.0)

to fight would be seriously affected; and conversely, other Native American tribes would be impressed by the Wampanoag successes, and would send their own warriors to support the war against the colonists. There was little chance that many Massachusetts or Mohegans would fight against the English, or Pequots or Niantics. The Nashaways and other Nipmuc nations, and the Norwottucks and other Pocumtucs, however, were eager to fight, and also the Podunks. It also was possible that more distant Mahican or Abenaki warriors might join in the war. What mattered most was whether the Narragansett nations, the most numerous in New England, would fight with the Wampanoags.

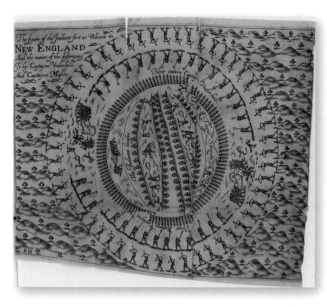

If enough warriors joined the Wampanoags. the colonists might be defeated. They would, however, confront an enemy that would greatly outnumber them. The Native American tribes of New England had a total population of roughly 10,000, of which 2,000 were Praying Indians. The Wampanoags totaled a mere 1,000, and could field about 250 warriors. The Narragansetts, the largest nation, had about 4,000, and could field about 1,000 warriors.

The settler population of New England, in contrast, totaled around 80,000 people, who lived in over 100 towns and large villages. Nearly 20,000 male colonists were of military age. All the major urban centers were protected with sturdily constructed garrison houses, while most minor settlements were enclosed within stockades and had at least one strong house. In addition, the settlers could count on the support of the Praying Indians, who could field about 200 warriors.

'The Figure of the Indians' Fort or Palizado in New England and the manner of the destroying It by Captayne Underhill and Captayne Mason,' from *Newes from America; or, A new and experimentall discoverie of New England; containing a true relation of their war-like proceedings these two yeares last past* (1638). This illustration shows the plan of attack on a fortified Pequot village in Mystic, Connecticut, in 1637, by colonists and their Narragansett allies (known as the Mystic Massacre). Although it dates from an earlier conflict, it provides clear details of the layout of a Native American settlement.

COLONIST

In 1675, the colonial authorities of New England were not expecting to be attacked by Native American warriors, but they were at least aware that Metacomet was very different from his father Massasoit. Some of the oldest settlers had fought in the Pequot War 37 years before. But the others had little understanding of what a war with Metacomet's warriors would be like. Although some had military experience in the English Civil War, and others had fought in Cromwell's wars in Scotland and Ireland, most had no experience with firearms beyond hunting.

The reaction to the attacks was not the uncontrolled panic that might have been expected from immigrant farmers and their families, for they were Puritans. The attacks, they assumed, were a test by God. Metacomet's warriors were not other men with grievances, with whom they could negotiate a peaceful resolution of a conflict. They were, as the cruelty they displayed to their enemies showed, heathen agents of the Devil.

The Puritans' reaction was to search for the war's cause, which must comprise actions by them that had offended God. It was, concluded Increase

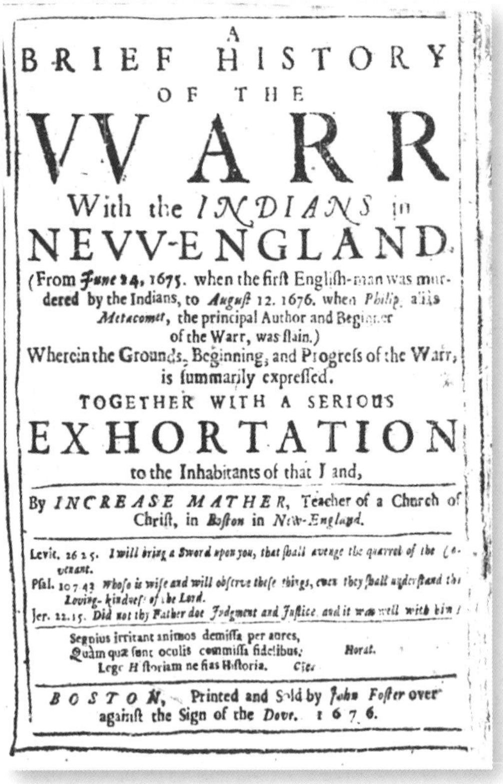

A
BRIEF HISTORY
OF THE
VVARR
With the INDIANS in
NEVV-ENGLAND.
(From June 24, 1675. when the first English-man was murdered by the Indians, to August 12. 1676. when Philip, alias Metacomet, the principal Author and Beginner of the Warr, was slain.)
Wherein the Grounds, Beginning, and Progress of the Warr, is summarily expressed.
TOGETHER WITH A SERIOUS
EXHORTATION
to the Inhabitants of that Land,
By INCREASE MATHER, Teacher of a Church of Christ, in Boston in New-England.

Levit. 26 25. I will bring a Sword upon you, that shall avenge the quarrel of the Covenant.
Psal. 107 43 Whoso is wise and will observe these things, even they shall understand the Loving-kindness of the Lord.
Jer. 22.15. Did not thy Father doe Judgment and Justice, and it was well with him?

Segnius irritant animos demissa per aures,
Quàm quæ sunt oculis commissa fidelibus. Horat.
Lege Historiam ne fias Historia. Cic.

BOSTON, Printed and Sold by John Foster over against the Sign of the Dove. 1676.

The frontispiece of Increase Mather's *A Brief History of the War with the Indians in New-England*, published in Boston during 1676. This work is a key primary source for the events of King Philip's War. Mather's account runs through August 1676, when hostilities in southern, central, and western New England ended. Mather claims his history to be both "brief" and "impartial," and although he was not a direct participant, his candid account was written at the time of the conflict. (Public domain)

Mather, New England's most celebrated minister, that they had failed to obey the mandates of their faith with the fidelity of their forefathers. He urged the Massachusetts legislature to adopt the "Provoking Evil Laws," which more strictly regulated dress, behavior, and church attendance. He later would see its cause in greed. "Land," he would write, "hath been the idol of many in New England. Whereas the first planters here, that they might keep themselves together, were satisfied with one acre for each person, as his propriety, and after that with twenty acres for a family, how have men since coveted after the earth, that many hundreds, nay thousands of acres, have been engrossed by one man, and they that profess themselves Christians have forsaken churches and ordinances, and all for land."

Although the Puritans' faith shaped every aspect of their plans, the colonists also were practical men. At the outbreak of hostilities, the colonists lacked a clear strategy to counter the threat of Native American incursions. Many settlements were too small and too remote to be defended effectively. The militia also lacked any fast-moving force that could strike against Native American villages in retaliation for Metacomet's raids. For these reasons, the settlers therefore adopted a defensive posture during the early part of the war, and sought to fend off the attacks as best as they could. Many of the smaller colonist settlements were abandoned, and their inhabitants were relocated to the larger towns. Large amounts of supplies and food were stockpiled in the major urban centers, and fortifications were strengthened and improved in more exposed locations. Emissaries were sent to the Narragansetts, Nipmucs, and other nations, urging them not to join Metacomet.

As the war progressed, the availability of Church's rangers and the loyal Mohegans improved the colonists' offensive capabilities, and they began planning retaliatory raids and attacks. But even if those efforts failed to end the war, the colonists would remain confident, for they would have an enormous strategic advantage in a continuing war of attrition. They had uncontested command of the sea.

From Portsmouth in the north to New Haven in the west, they had coastal strongholds that no Native American army could take. Although small settlements might be burned, larger towns, if adequately fortified and garrisoned, could not be stormed. Nor, because of the colonists' command of the sea, could they be taken by siege.

King Philip's War broke out in summer, a season during which the colonists could fight more or less on equal terms against the Native Americans. The following winter, however, the settlers experienced serious difficulties caused by the harsh climate. Unlike the natives, who needed fewer resources to survive during the cold months, the colonists needed large amounts of food and supplies to feed their families during winter. These had to be produced during summer and then placed into storage. The attacks of the previous summer, however, meant that the colonists had not been able to work in their plantations and thus had not produced sufficient food to tide them over.

Luckily for most of them, there were sufficient reserves stored from previous years, and thus the settlers could survive in this virtual state of siege for several months.

When the Narragansetts, Nipmucs, and other nations joined Metacomet, and the full scope of the threat they posed became clear, the New England colonists sent emissaries to England asking for aid. They would receive no response. King Charles II disliked the New England colonists, who had always opposed his rule. But if no ships would arrive carrying soldiers from England, vessels with other cargos would continue to appear from ports in England, the English colonies, and elsewhere.

Both the Native Americans and the colonists could fight only if they had adequate supplies of food and munitions. The Native Americans obtained most of their food from farming and hunting. As English and allied Native American raiders burned their crops, and their hunters were continually diverted to service as warriors, their available food would diminish. The Native Americans also were completely dependent on the English for supplies of munitions. As the colonists abandoned indefensible settlements, the ability of the Native Americans to replenish their supplies from captured stocks of powder and balls also would wane.

The colonists, in contrast, would never starve or face enemies unarmed. They might suffer shortages. They would, moreover, pay high prices to attract the ships bringing what they needed. But the food and munitions would continue to arrive.

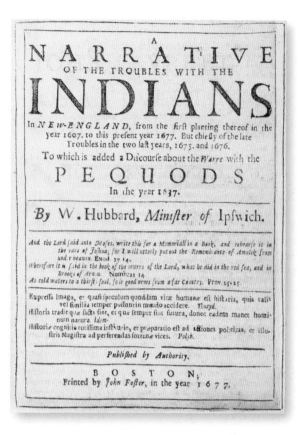

The frontispiece for *A Narrative of the Troubles with the Indians in New-England*, by William Hubbard (1621–1704), first printed in 1677. Hubbard was born in Ipswich, UK, and emigrated with his parents to New England as a child. Among his other works are a *History of New England*, a work commissioned by the colonial authorities. (Public domain)

McIntire Garrison House, located in York, MA, is a rare example of a well-preserved New England garrison house. Built in 1707, it was specifically designed to protect against Native American raids. Its walls are 19cm thick and dovetailed together at the corners. (Wikimedia Commons/ Magicpiano, CC BY-SA 3.0)

THE CAMPAIGN

THE RAID ON SWANSEA AND THE OPENING ATTACKS

On June 20, 1675, a small war band of Wampanoags attacked the frontier settlement of Swansea, located some ten miles northeast of Metacomet's main base of Mount Hope (modern Bristol, RI). Several colonist homes were looted and two of them were set on fire. The few settlers, isolated as they were, had no choice but to flee for their lives.

A messenger was sent to Marshfield to inform Governor Winslow, who soon sent orders to the settlements of Bridgewater and Taunton to ready a force of 200 militiamen. These would move to the Swansea area to protect it from further attack. The colonists from Swansea who had abandoned their homes were moved to better-protected locations, such as the Bourne garrison house at Mattapoisett and the Miles garrison house at the head of the Pokanoket Peninsula.

The colonial authorities now made concerted efforts to prevent further tribes from joining forces with King Philip and taking arms against the New England settlements. In Boston, the fear was that the Nipmucs, a powerful local tribe who dominated the terrain to the west of the settlement, might ally themselves with Metacomet and attack the Massachusetts Bay capital. The decision was taken to send a negotiating party to the Nipmucs, which was led by the young Ephraim Curtis. His orders were to meet with the Nipmuc chiefs and obtain clear promises of loyalty from them. The negotiating party advanced deep into Native American territory, but found the Nipmuc villages deserted; Curtis was able to find out later, from a captured hostile Native American, that the Nipmucs were holding a war council at a secret location, which the colonists were able to extract from their prisoner. They arrived at the council while the meeting was still taking place, and Curtis was able to address the Nipmuc leaders. They promised him that they would never form an alliance with Metacomet, and so Ephraim Curtis began his journey back to Boston with this encouraging news.

The early seal of Massachusetts Bay Colony, taken from Increase Mather's *A Brief History of the War with the Indians in New-England* (1676). It was in use from 1629 to 1684. The words the Native American is speaking, "Come Over and Help Us," reflect the early missionary aims of the colony. (Courtesy of the John Carter Brown Library, CC BY-SA 4.0)

By June 24, the 200 militiamen assembled from Bridgewater and Taunton had reached Swansea, and had occupied the local garrison house; they were too few, however, to protect the whole area and all of its scattered settlements. Many of Swansea's inhabitants, in fact, were in the process of returning to their homes to gather up food and other supplies. Moving without escorts, many of them were ambushed and killed by Native American warriors who were roaming throughout the surrounding area.

While these events took place between colonist areas and Wampanoag territory, the Massachusetts Bay authorities called to arms several militia companies and sent them to the aid of the colonists in and around Swansea. After receiving these reinforcements, the militiamen in the area decided to move on Metacomet's base at Mount Hope on the Pokanoket Peninsula. They headed southwest without meeting any resistance, and when they arrived at Mount Hope, they found that King Philip and his followers had already fled across Mount Hope Bay into Pocasset Country. Captain Thomas Savage, commander of the militiamen, opted to stop at Mount Hope in order to construct a fort, rather than pursuing Metacomet and his warrior band.

The colonial authorities in both Boston and Plymouth were also concerned about the possibility of the powerful Narragansetts joining forces with Metacomet's warriors. They sent a negotiating party to the Narragansetts, led by Captain Edward Hutchinson, who was accompanied by several Massachusetts militiamen from the Swansea area as a bodyguard. When Hutchinson arrived at the main Narragansett camp, he found the atmosphere to be laden with tension; it appears the tribe had already decided to side with King Philip, and were attempting to provoke the militiamen in every possible way. Hutchinson acted with sound intelligence, avoiding any attempts to force the Native Americans to accept a new treaty, and was able to leave with his men without harm coming to them.

As June 1675 drew to a close, Wampanoag warriors began to make their hostile presence felt in other settler areas. They attacked Taunton on June 27, and Old Rehoboth a few days later. On July 9, they raided the settlement of Middleborough and burned it to the ground. Dartmouth was also attacked. After decades of peace and stability, the attacks on the New England settlements, which had expanded in a largely peaceful environment, came as a shock, and even a handful of Native American warriors were enough to destroy some of them.

Within a few weeks of war breaking out, it became clear that the Narragansetts and Nipmucs would ally themselves with King Philip's cause. The former launched a raid against Providence, RI, while the latter conducted an attack against Mendon, in Massachusetts Bay Colony. Less than a month from the start of the conflict, it was already spreading from Plymouth Colony to Rhode Island and Massachusetts. The diplomatic missions to the Nipmucs and Narragansetts had evidently failed in their objectives, and there was a growing sense that many of the New England settlements were in the process of being surrounded by hostile Native Americans.

When Captain Hutchinson integrated the men under his command with the militiamen deployed in the Pokanoket Peninsula, the colonists decided to move in force against King Philip's positions in Pocasset Country. Having marched to his base, the colonists found only an abandoned camp; a few skirmishes were fought with a Wampanoag rear-guard of warriors, but the Native Americans did not pause in their withdrawal and avoided any

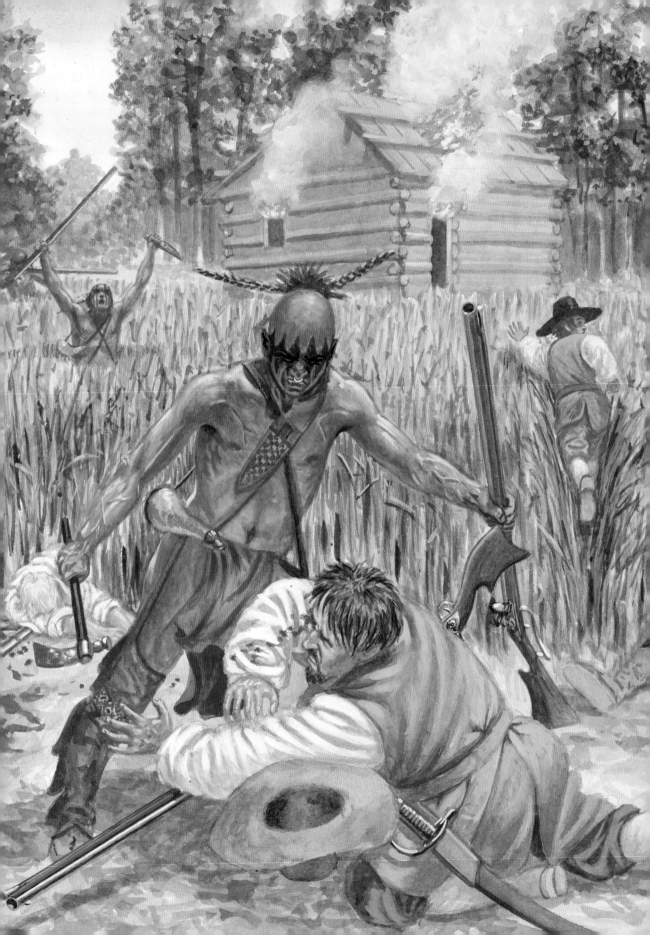

THE ATTACK ON SWANSEA, JUNE 20–25, 1675 (PP. 44–45)

Swansea was the location of the first bloodshed of King Philip's War. Prior to the war, the site had been home to several Native American settlements. The first colonists arrived there in 1663. The settlement was named for a town in Wales, from which its minister hailed. The land of the settlement was conveyed in 1664 to William Brenton of Newport. By June 1675, it was home to some 70 settlers, and the town had one stronghouse. A further garrison house was located about half a mile to the south of Swansea, occupied by Jared Bourne.

On June 20, 1675, a warrior band attacked and looted the homes of some of the settlers at Swansea, setting two of them alight, including Hugh Cole's house. The inhabitants retreated to the safety of the settlement's stockade. The warriors returned to attack Swansea again over the following days, looting and burning further settler houses. One of the settlers defending Swansea was William Salsbury; Salsbury (**1**), his son John, and seven other settlers, would become the first colonist victims of the war, killed on June 24 by Native American warriors (**2**). Increase Mather wrote of this day: "Thus did the war begin, this being the first English blood which was spilt by the Indians in an hostile way … the Lord thereby declaring from heaven that he expects something else from his People besides fasting and prayer."

By June 25, all of Swansea had been burned down. A handful of settlers managed to escape to Taunton. Swansea would be rebuilt and resettled after the war.

direct confrontation with the militiamen. Using their excellent mobility and knowledge of the terrain, the Wampanoags managed to kill or wound several militiamen without suffering any losses. The pursuit took place in the challenging terrain of Pocasset Swamp—a huge cedar bog—which the Wampanoags crossed with greater ease than the colonists. Realizing it was pointless to attempt to cut off Metacomet's withdrawal, the militiamen opted to cease their pursuit of the Wampanoags.

A new defensive position, named Fort Leverett for the Governor of Massachusetts Bay Colony, was built to the southwest of Pocasset Swamp, to cover any movement by water through this area. A few militiamen were left behind in the Pocasset area, to harass the Wampanoags and destroy their access to food supplies.

On July 29, however, the militiamen left their positions just outside Pocasset Swamp in order to come to the aid of the town of Dartmouth, lying some 20 miles east of Mount Hope, which had come under Native American attack. King Philip, however, had taken the opportunity to slip across the Taunton River and was moving northeast toward Old Rehoboth. His objective was to enter Nipmuc territory, where he would be safe. The Wampanoag sachem had escaped the trap that the colonists had set for him, but the price paid was that more than 100 Wampanoag women and children were abandoned in Pocasset Swamp. They were later captured by militiamen, and most were sold into slavery.

The threat to King Philip did not only come from the colonists. A large force of Mohegans, allies of the settlers, was tracking him, under the command of the war chief Oneko. The Mohegans had been sent from Connecticut Colony to help in the pursuit of Metacomet, and proved to be much more efficient than the militiamen in pursuing and catching up with the Wampanoags. On August 1, 1675, the Mohegans, supported by a number of colonist militiamen, clashed briefly but violently with King Philip and his warriors at Nipsachuc (Nipsachuck Swamp, RI). The Wampanoags lost 23 men during the battle, including four senior, experienced warriors.

The Miles Garrison House in Swansea, as it looked at the beginning of the 20th century. The stronghouse belonged to the Reverend Miles, a Baptist clergyman. It was the location of the first meeting of troops from Massachusetts Bay and Plymouth colonies under the command of majors Thomas Savage and James Cudworth, as they marched to the relief of Swansea at the opening of the war. It stood a short distance from the bridge leading to Mount Hope. The photo is taken from *King Philip's War* by Ellis and Morris, published in 1906. (Public domain)

Metacomet's band of warriors was reduced to just 40 men, who were at risk of being surrounded by the 250-strong militia–Mohegan force. Yet King Philip was able to escape once again, haven taken shelter alongside his remaining men in a nearby swamp, from which he later fled along the course of the Blackstone River. The Wampanoags eventually entered Nipmuc territory, where they joined forces with their allies.

The colonists missed a major opportunity to halt Metacomet during this early phase of the war, before he was able to unite his forces with other hostile native tribes. The militiamen had moved too slowly and without sufficient aggression; despite their superior numbers, they had not been able to catch King Philip's band and had covered a large number of miles without much to show for it. Metacomet, however, had shown the other native chiefs that he was a trustworthy and skilled sachem, whose warriors had destroyed several enemy settlements without being intercepted by the colonists. At this point of the war, it was becoming clearer that conflict would soon begin to spread into other areas of New England and that much larger battles would take place than the modest clashes to date. The Native American warriors could rightly feel elated at the results so far: after decades of submission and passivity, a great leader had arisen in Metacomet. On June 27, 1675, a full eclipse of the moon took place in the skies of New England—interpreted by many Native Americans as a good omen for the launching of all-out war against the colonists.

WHEELER'S SURPRISE AND THE SIEGE OF BROOKFIELD

On July 14, 1675, the colonist settlement of Mendon in Massachusetts Bay Colony was attacked by a band of Nipmuc warriors led by Matoonas, whose son had been put to death on questionable evidence by the colonial authorities four years earlier. Several settlers were killed. This raised panic among colonists throughout Nipmuc territory, for it was clear that pro-Metacomet tendencies were coming to the fore among the Nipmuc tribe; it also indicated that the conflict was beginning to spread. This was the first attack of the war to take place outside of Plymouth Colony territory.

Just prior to the attack on Mendon, the Boston authorities made attempts to guarantee a pro-colonist position of the Nipmucs, and decided to send a negotiating party into Nipmuc territory to seek out their chief Muttawmp. The party was led by Lieutenant Ephraim Curtis, with an escort of militiamen. By the time his party had entered Nipmuc territory and located Muttawmp (July 14), the attack on Mendon was already underway, and the Nipmucs had already sided with Metacomet—but Curtis remained unaware of this. Muttawmp feigned friendliness, and stated that he would visit Boston in a week's time to show loyalty. Curtis then returned to Boston to relate what he had been told.

Instead of waiting for Muttawmp to show himself in Boston, the colonial authorities dispatched a further militia force under Captain Edward Hutchinson and Captain Thomas Wheeler into Nipmuc territory, seeking to negotiate directly with the sachem. Some 25 mounted militiamen accompanied them, along with Native American guides, and Ephraim Curtis. Wheeler's men reached the main Nipmuc base on July 31, but the village was found to be deserted. At this point, the Native American guides, who were "Natick praying Indians," tried to persuade the colonists to withdraw for fear of a surprise attack by the Nipmucs. Hutchinson and Wheeler, however, decided to continue their advance and sent Curtis in search of the leading Nipmucs. These were located after several hours of searching, and only with great difficulty, since they had moved to a village some distance from their usual settlement. Curtis was able to arrange a meeting with all the Nipmuc chiefs for the following day, at the new camp.

On August 2, as agreed, the militiamen advanced towards the place where Curtis had encountered the Native Americans the previous day. In order to reach the new Nipmuc camp, the colonists had to cross a swamp along a narrow path, strung out in single file. Once again, the Natick guides warned of the threat of ambush by the Nipmucs, but Hutchinson and Wheeler decided to push on. After marching some 300 yards through the swamp, the militiamen were ambushed by Nipmuc warriors hiding in the tall grass that surrounded the narrow path. The Native Americans did not charge the militiamen, but fired on them with muskets and bows from close range; at this point the colonists turned back and tried to move back along the narrow path, but soon found another group of Nipmuc warriors blocking their retreat.

Hutchinson and Wheeler were badly wounded in the attack, alongside several of their men, and eight colonists were killed. The militiamen had been caught in the open, and the attack had been so rapid that they were unable to return fire. The few survivors were saved by their Native American guides, who took over from the wounded captains and led the remaining militiamen out of the swamp and into the nearby hills. Muttawmp had organized a perfect ambush, but the colonists had also been the authors of their own misfortune. The colonist survivors headed quickly for the nearby settlement of Brookfield, with Muttawmp and his warriors in close pursuit.

Brookfield

The village of Brookfield, at that time known by the native name of Quabaug, was isolated and comprised just 20 houses. Following the arrival of the militiamen who had survived the ambush, its inhabitants decided to gather together in the largest, most robust building in the settlement: the house of John Ayres, a sergeant of the local militia who had accompanied Wheeler and Hutchinson on their mission to negotiate with the Nipmucs and who had been killed during the ambush later known as Wheeler's Surprise. In total, 80 people assembled in Ayres' house and prepared to kill or be killed by the fast-approaching Nipmucs.

Ephraim Curtis and another man were given horses and were sent to

A 19th-century depiction of Muttawmp's attack on Brookfield. The settlement's few inhabitants gathered in the only fortified house for protection, while the Native Americans burned down the other buildings. (Public domain)

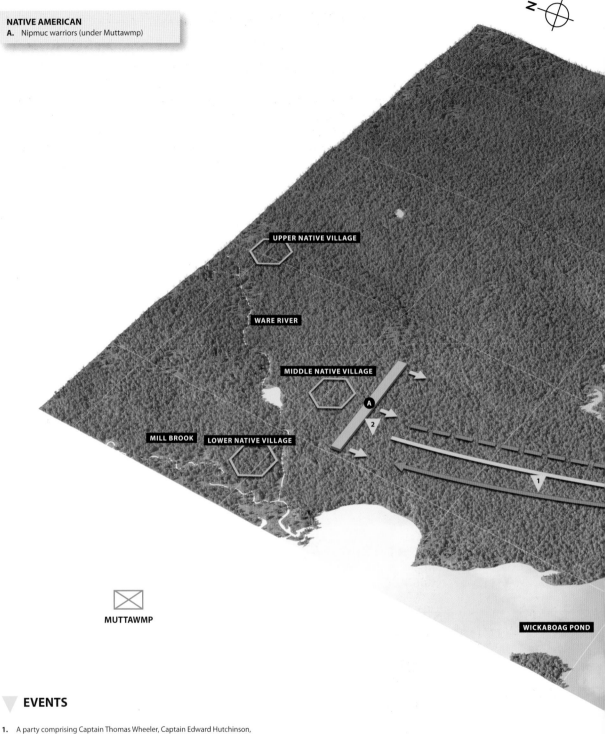

N

UPPER NATIVE VILLAGE

WARE RIVER

MIDDLE NATIVE VILLAGE

A

2

MILL BROOK

LOWER NATIVE VILLAGE

1

MUTTAWMP

WICKABOAG POND

▼ EVENTS

1. A party comprising Captain Thomas Wheeler, Captain Edward Hutchinson, Ephraim Curtis, 25 militiamen, and allied Native American guides enters Nipmuc territory to negotiate with the tribal leaders.

2. Before reaching the lower Native American village close to the Ware River, Wheeler's column is ambushed and attacked by a large number of Nipmuc warriors led by the sachem Muttawmp.

3. The colonists are taken by surprise and struggle to organize their resistance. Eight militiamen are killed in the ambush, and both Wheeler and Hutchinson are badly wounded. Led by their Native American guides, the remains of Wheeler's column are forced back to Brookfield, pursued by the Nipmuc warriors.

4. As the militiamen and pursuing Native Americans reach Brookfield, Muttawmp's warriors begin to attack the colonial settlement.

5. The Native American warriors destroy all the houses in Brookfield, but are unable to reduce the settlement's only fortified building, its garrison house.

6. Brookfield's besieged colonists and Wheeler's men are saved by the arrival of reinforcements from Lancaster under the command of 70-year-old Major Simon Willard, late in the evening of August 3.

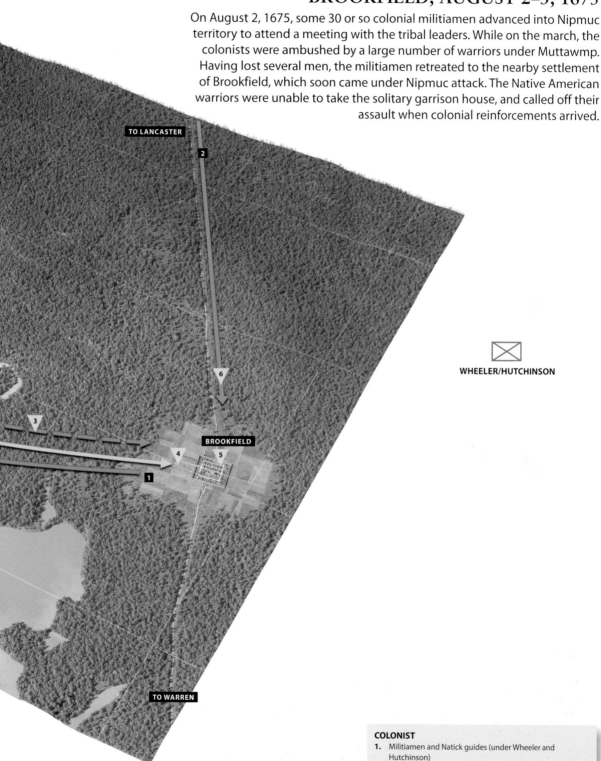

WHEELER'S SURPRISE AND THE SIEGE OF BROOKFIELD, AUGUST 2–3, 1675

On August 2, 1675, some 30 or so colonial militiamen advanced into Nipmuc territory to attend a meeting with the tribal leaders. While on the march, the colonists were ambushed by a large number of warriors under Muttawmp. Having lost several men, the militiamen retreated to the nearby settlement of Brookfield, which soon came under Nipmuc attack. The Native American warriors were unable to take the solitary garrison house, and called off their assault when colonial reinforcements arrived.

WHEELER/HUTCHINSON

TO LANCASTER

BROOKFIELD

TO WARREN

Note: gridlines are shown at intervals of 1km (0.62 miles)

COLONIST
1. Militiamen and Natick guides (under Wheeler and Hutchinson)
2. Reinforcements from Lancaster (under Major Simon Willard)

A 19th-century engraving of the crucial moment in the Siege of Brookfield, when Muttawmp's warriors set a cart alight and drove it against the stronghouse. Their efforts came to nothing when the flames were extinguished by rain. (Public domain)

Marlborough to bring help. Before they had traveled far from Brookfield, the two men were intercepted by Muttawmp's warriors, who had already surrounded the village. Curtis was forced to turn back to Brookfield and warned the defenders that the Nipmuc attack was imminent.

As soon as they arrived in Brookfield, the Native American warriors burned down all the houses that had been left undefended by the colonists. Then they surrounded Ayres' house, and continued to fire upon it with their muskets and bows for the next 48 hours. They also tried to set fire to it using poles with burning rags dipped in brimstone tied to the ends.

When it became clear that these were not working, Muttawmp ordered a cart to be filled with all available combustible material (birch bark, straw, black powder) and set alight. It was then pushed towards the house using long poles. However, with the flaming cart barely lit, a sudden downpour fell on Brookfield, extinguished the flames, and soaked the material in the cart.

The colonists offered stubborn resistance, but several of them were killed or wounded by Native American fire penetrating the building's windows. Cut off from stocks of water, food, and ammunition, the fate of the surrounded Brookfield colonists looked grim.

On August 3, however, taking advantage of a lull in the fighting, Ephraim Curtis managed to escape from the house and made his way through the Nipmuc lines without being captured. He made for Marlborough (30 miles from Brookfield) on foot, moving as fast as he could. Before Curtis got there, however, some unexpected reinforcements reached the settlement. These comprised 48 militiamen under command of Major Simon Willard, who were already operating against the Native Americans west of Lancaster. They had been informed of the attack on Brookfield by some people traveling through the area who had heard the sound of intense musket fire.

Willard's men arrived at Brookfield after nightfall on August 3, and at first the Nipmuc warriors were unaware of the presence of this relief expedition.

Willard's men were thus able to enter Ayres' house and bring ammunition to the surviving defenders. At this point, Muttawmp, realizing that the enemy position had been reinforced, decided to break off the attack and withdraw.

Soon after the Native Americans left Brookfield, further large numbers of colonial reinforcements reached the village. These brought the total number of men under Willard's command to 350, and also included the Mohegan warriors who had fought King Philip at Nipsachuc. Although Brookfield was now garrisoned in strength, the local inhabitants had lost most of their property and decided to abandon the settlement.

THE WAR SPREADS

On August 5, 1675, King Philip's warriors joined forces with those of Muttawmp, at the newly built Nipmuc camp at Menameset. Metacomet's escape from the pursuing Mohegans, and Muttawmp's successful ambush, had galvanized many of the Native Americans of New England; as a result, an increasing number of warriors from different communities started to gather at Menameset.

On August 22, a Native American warrior band attacked Lancaster in Massachusetts, killing seven colonists and burning down one of its houses. In an effort to prevent the war spreading westward into Connecticut Colony, a large, combined military force was assembled at Hadley comprising Massachusetts and Connecticut militiamen, plus allied Mohegan warriors. Along the western bank of the Connecticut River, above the colonial settlement of Northampton, Norwottuck warriors were gathering in increasing numbers, despite the apparently neutral position adopted by the tribal leaders. A Norwottuck attack in that area, if it materialized, could prove a worrying development.

As a result, on August 24, the colonists held a council of war at Hatfield and decided to send a force of 100 militiamen under the command of captains

The Hopewell Swamp in the early 1900s, looking north to Mount Sugarloaf, near South Deerfield, MA, in the Connecticut River Valley. On August 25, 1675, Massachusetts Bay militiamen clashed with Norwottuck warriors there. This photo is taken from *King Philip's War* by Ellis and Morris, published in 1906. (Public domain)

Thomas Lathrop and Richard Beers to surprise and disarm the Norwottucks before they could strike. Native scouts, however, gave word to their fellow tribesmen of the colonist advance, and the Norwottucks abandoned their camp shortly before the arrival of the militiamen.

At this point, Lathrop and Beers split their force, sending part of it back to Hatfield while continuing to move forward after the Norwottucks with the rest. One mile south of present-day South Deerfield, the militiamen finally caught up with the Norwottucks, who then spread out into the nearby Hopewell Swamp and then set an ambush for the advancing militiamen. The ensuing events were similar to those of Wheeler's Surprise, but on this occasion, the colonists were able to return fire and killed some of the Native Americans. At the end of three hours of fighting, the settlers had lost nine men and the Norwottucks around 20.

THE NORTHERN THEATER: MAINE

By this date, there also was fighting far to the north in Maine, where New England settlers were living near the Abenakis. Among the Abenakis were French traders and priests. In contrast to the English settlers, the French in the area had little interest in permanent colonization in Maine. They instead sought to control the fur trade in the area.

The Abenakis did not see the French as a threat to their autonomy, because the latter were few in number. They had, moreover, much to gain from good commercial links with the French. When the French urged the Abenakis to expel the English colonists in southern Maine, the Abenakis attacked. The French, led by Jean-Vincent d'Abbadie de Saint-Castin, supplied muskets and powder, and joined in the assault.

The colonists, led by Richard Waldron and Charles Frost, defended the settlements. Because this fighting arose in circumstances unrelated to King Philip's insurrection, and the French and Abenaki operations were completely independent of those to the south, it is often considered a separate conflict, sometimes called the First Abenaki War. Given that it coincided in time with Metacomet's operations, however, it is sometimes considered a theater of King Philip's War.

It began soon after the opening Wampanoag attack on Swansea. The English colonists in Maine, alarmed at rumors that the Abenakis were talking about war, marched to the Sheepscot River to demand that the nearest, the Androscoggins, surrender their weapons. The Androscoggins, who used their muskets for hunting, refused. The colonists then unsuccessfully attempted to take the weapons by force.

On September 5, 1675, the Androscoggins responded to the settlers' actions by raiding a trading post at Topsham and killing several heads of cattle. Falmouth was raided on September 12, with several colonists killed. On September 18, the Sokokis joined their fellow Abenakis. Led by their sachem Squandro, the Sokokis launched a series of attacks against isolated colonist settlements near the Saco River. Many colonists abandoned their houses and took shelter in the local garrison house at Biddeford Falls, commanded by Major William Philips, who also owned a mill there. Squandro's attack on the garrison house was repulsed, but Philips' mill was burnt down. During October, before the native warriors would retreat to their winter quarters,

Beers' Ambush

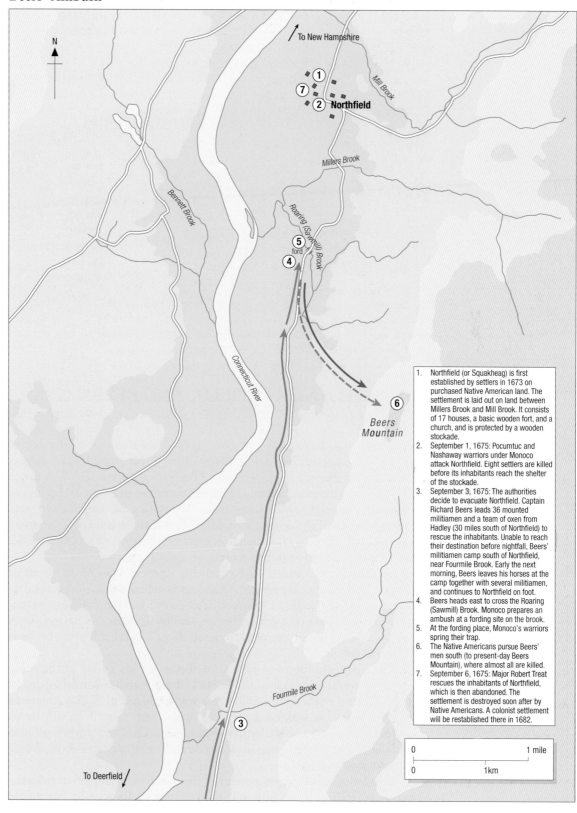

N

To New Hampshire

Mill Brook

① Northfield ⑦ ②

Millers Brook

Roaring (Sawmill) Brook

⑤ ford ④

Bennett Brook

Connecticut River

⑥

Beers Mountain

③

Fourmile Brook

To Deerfield

1. Northfield (or Squakheag) is first established by settlers in 1673 on purchased Native American land. The settlement is laid out on land between Millers Brook and Mill Brook. It consists of 17 houses, a basic wooden fort, and a church, and is protected by a wooden stockade.
2. September 1, 1675: Pocumtuc and Nashaway warriors under Monoco attack Northfield. Eight settlers are killed before its inhabitants reach the shelter of the stockade.
3. September 3, 1675: The authorities decide to evacuate Northfield. Captain Richard Beers leads 36 mounted militiamen and a team of oxen from Hadley (30 miles south of Northfield) to rescue the inhabitants. Unable to reach their destination before nightfall, Beers' militiamen camp south of Northfield, near Fourmile Brook. Early the next morning, Beers leaves his horses at the camp together with several militiamen, and continues to Northfield on foot.
4. Beers heads east to cross the Roaring (Sawmill) Brook. Monoco prepares an ambush at a fording site on the brook.
5. At the fording place, Monoco's warriors spring their trap.
6. The Native Americans pursue Beers' men south (to present-day Beers Mountain), where almost all are killed.
7. September 6, 1675: Major Robert Treat rescues the inhabitants of Northfield, which is then abandoned. The settlement is destroyed soon after by Native Americans. A colonist settlement will be restablished there in 1682.

| 0 | | 1 mile |
| 0 | 1km | |

several isolated outposts in the Saco River area were assaulted and most of their owners were massacred.

DEERFIELD, NORTHFIELD, AND BEERS' AMBUSH

On September 1, 1675, 60 warriors attacked the colonial settlement of Deerfield in the upper Connecticut River Valley. Most of the local buildings and barns were burned to the ground. The Native Americans' next target was the nearby village of Northfield, which consisted of about 20 buildings. Northfield's inhabitants were unaware of the attack on Deerfield, and were taken by surprise. Eight settlers were killed before the members of the small community managed to take shelter behind the settlement's stockade, from where they watched their houses burn.

On hearing of the attack on Northfield, an expedition of 36 mounted militiamen, under the command of Captain Richard Beers, and a team of oxen set out from Hadley (30 miles from Northfield) to come to its aid. Unable to reach their destination before sundown, Beers' militiamen were forced to camp around four miles to the south of Northfield, probably next to Fourmile Brook.

In the early morning of September 4, Beers left his horses at the camp along with several militiamen, and continued the march toward Northfield on foot. Aware that the surrounding area was likely full of Native American warriors waiting to ambush his force, Beers' men moved as silently as possible. His men advanced along the main route, until they turned off it to follow the course of the Sawmill (today known as Roaring) Brook, which flowed through a ravine.

Having followed the brook upstream, the colonists attempted to cross the Sawmill at a fording point normally used by those approaching Northfield from the south. The Native Americans, who had been shadowing the militiamen for several hours and saw where they were heading, set a deadly trap at the ford; at this point, the whole of the column would be exposed to fire as it moved into the open to cross the water. As Beers' men entered the Sawmill, the Native Americans concealed behind a steep bank below the crossing place sprang up and fired on the column of men. At first, the colonists were taken by surprise, but managed to fight their way out of the ravine, and made a stand after retreating south. The natives, however, followed them in close pursuit: in the end Captain Beers and a few survivors retreated further south and attempted to shelter in a small ravine three-quarters of a mile on a southern spur of modern Beers Mountain. They resisted as best they could, but were all killed, including Beers, whose grave is located there. The men who had been left with the horses returned to Hadley that evening, along with the few survivors of the ambush—a total of 13 militiamen. In total, 21 colonists were killed. Over the next few days, several stragglers who had also escaped managed to make it back.

Beers' Ambush had a devastating effect on the morale of the colonists. In addition, the expedition had failed to reach the terrified inhabitants of Northfield, who remained within the settlement's stockade. On September 6, a force of 100 militiamen under the command of Major Robert Treat (who had accompanied Beers, and managed to escape back to Hadley) finally got through to the civilians of Northfield. En route, they had to pass the gruesome sight of the decapitated heads of slain settlers strung up by their enemy. Once its stores of food had been gathered up (to both feed the settler

The monument stone at the location of Beers' Ambush, near Northfield, MA. (Watertown Free Public Library)

The location of Beers' Ambush as it appears today. (Photo courtesy of Eric B. Schultz)

BLOODY BROOK, SEPTEMBER 18, 1675 (PP. 58–59)

On September 18, 1675, Captain Thomas Lathrop and a force of just under 80 militiamen were on their way back to Hadley from Deerfield, escorting the latter settlement's evacuating inhabitants and their "Carts loaden with Goods and Provision" (**1**). At a certain point, the colonists paused to rest near a shallow brook, a few miles south of Deerfield. The Native American sachem Muttawmp chose this moment to launch "a sudden and frightful assault" on the colonists with his Nipmuc warriors (**2**).

Increase Mather records: "They seized upon the Carts and Goods (many of the Souldiers having been so foolish and secure, as to put their Arms in the Carts, and step aside to gather Grapes, which proved dear and deadly Grapes to them) killed Captain Lathrop, and above threescore of his men, stripped them of their clothes, and so left them to lye weltring in their own Blood."

A party of militiamen under Captain Mosely had earlier been dispatched into the woods to check for Native American warriors, and hearing the sound of gunfire, quickly hurried back to the brook—but too late to save Lathrop and many of his men.

"Nevertheless he gave the Indians Battle : they were in such numbers, as that he and his company were in extream danger, the Indians endeavouring (according to their mode of fighting) to encompass the English round, and then to press in upon them with great numbers, so to knock them down with their Hatchets." Despite the danger, only a few of Moseley's men were killed.

When a large body of colonial reinforcements and Native American allies under Major Robert Treat arrived at the brook, Muttawmp and his Nipmuc warriors withdrew, having executed a bloody and significant massacre. Mather records the Nipmuc deaths as "ninety six men that day, and that they had above forty wounded, many of which dyed afterwards."

The Battle of Bloody Brook was, in the words of Mather, "a black and fatal day, wherein there were eight persons made Widows, and six and twenty Children made Fatherless, all in one little Plantation, and in one day; and above sixty Persons buried in one dreadful Grave."

The location of the Battle of Bloody Brook, from *King Philip's War* (1906). A monument commemorating the engagement can be seen to the right of the building, in the background. (Public domain)

refugees and prevent them falling into Native American hands), Northfield was abandoned and left to be destroyed by the Native Americans, who made no attempts to attack Treat's force.

THE BATTLE OF BLOODY BROOK

On September 12, a few days after the evacuation of Northfield, Deerfield was attacked for the second time by a small band of Native American warriors. They destroyed two houses and carried off several wagons full of food supplies. The Massachusetts Bay authorities decided that the evacuation of Deerfield was also required, given that it was now exposed after the abandonment of Northfield. The fall harvest of that year had been excellent, and thus the settlement was well stocked with food supplies that the colonists would need to survive the following winter. Captain Thomas Lathrop and a force of militiamen were thus dispatched to Deerfield, with orders to evacuate its inhabitants and escort them to Hadley together with the recently harvested food stocks.

Having carried out his orders, Lathrop departed Deerfield on September 18, escorting a long convoy of carts filled with provisions; he had a total of 79 militiamen under his command. During the

A 19th-century engraving of the Battle of Bloody Brook. The militiamen under Thomas Lathrop were caught by surprise by the Native Americans, as they rested by the shallow brook. (Public domain)

The monument at the location of the Battle of Bloody Brook, on North Main St, South Deerfield, MA. It was erected in August 1838. (Wikimedia Commons/Tom Walsh, CC BY-SA 3.0)

The inscription on the Bloody Brook monument. (Wikimedia Commons/Daderot, CC0 1.0)

On this Ground Capt. THOMAS LATHROP and eighty four men under his command including eighteen teamsters from Deerfield, conveying stores from that town to Hadley, were ambuscaded by about 700 Indians, and the Captain and seventy six men slain, September 18th 1675. (old style)

The soldiers who fell, were described by a cotemporary Historian, as "a choice Company of young men, the very flower of the County of Essex none of whom were ashamed to speak with the enemy in the gate."

"And SANGUINETTO tells you where the dead Made the earth wet and turned the unwilling waters red."

"The Same of the slain is marked by a Stone slab, 21 rods Southerly of this monument."

march toward Hadley, near a shallow brook located a few miles south of Deerfield, the first cart of the convoy paused to rest, waiting for the other carts following a little way behind to catch up. Some of the militiamen put down their arms to gather fruit and rest, too. The sachem Muttawmp and his Nipmuc warriors, who had tracked the movements of the convoy since its departure from Deerfield, chose this moment to attack the carts. Lathrop was killed almost immediately, and in the following massacre the colonists suffered 60 deaths (43 militiamen and 17 civilians). While in Deerfield, Lathrop had detached part of his men to probe the surrounding area in search of Native Americans. When fighting broke out, these men returned to aid the main column and entered a desperate fight with Muttawmp's warriors. Their efforts enabled the survivors from the main column to escape the battlefield and avoid being massacred. The Nipmucs abandoned the field of battle only when colonial reinforcements under command of Major Robert Treat arrived a few hours later.

The brook at which the colonists had stopped, known as Muddy Brook to that point, received the new moniker Bloody Brook. Muttawmp's warriors moved to Deerfield shortly after and destroyed the settlement. The Battle of Bloody Brook was the worst defeat suffered by the New England militia, and some 700 Native American warriors were involved in the clash. After the events of Bloody Brook, all the colonial settlements located in the Connecticut River Valley came under pressure to evacuate.

THE SIEGE OF SPRINGFIELD AND THE ATTACK ON HATFIELD

Springfield in Massachusetts was a prime target for an attack by King Philip's supporters. It was already an important center, with a population of 500 settlers, and was made up of four distinct villages. The town occupied a strategic position on the Connecticut River and at the junction of two important trails. Near Springfield lay a Native American village of the Agawam tribe. The Agawams had remained neutral after the outbreak of hostilities, but the colonists feared that they might ally with Metacomet and join in an attack on the town.

On October 4, 1675, most of Springfield's militiamen left the town to join a body of troops being assembled at Hadley in preparation for a move on a Native American camp. The threat of an attack at that time was considered to be low, and so only a small garrison was left in the town. This, however, proved a fatal mistake. In recent days, the supposedly neutral Agawams had given shelter to a large group of hostile warriors, who were poised to attack the colonist settlement. On the night of October 4, they were augmented by the arrival of several hundred additional warriors, ready to take advantage of this plentiful opportunity.

William Pynchon (1590–1662), the founder of Springfield, MA, in 1636. At first Springfield was known as "Agawam," but four years later was renamed Springfield after Pynchon's home village in Essex, England. (Public domain)

The attack was planned for the early morning of October 5. A Native American employed by a colonist family, however, became aware of the impending attack, and warned the settlers. The inhabitants of Springfield quickly sought shelter within the town's three garrison houses before the Native American warriors could launch their attack. Meanwhile, a messenger was rapidly sent to Hadley to recall the recently departed militiamen.

The Old Fort at Springfield, MA. The fort was built in 1657 by John Pynchon, the son of Springfield's founder William Pynchon. Its sturdy construction provided shelter to Springfield's inhabitants during the attack in October 1675. The building survived until 1831, when it was pulled down. (Public domain)

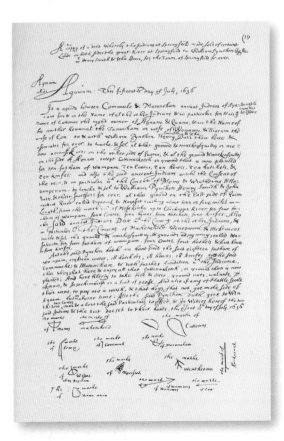

The 1636 deed between the colonists William Pynchon, Henry Smith, and Jehu Burr, and native tribesmen Menis, Machetuhood, Cuttonas, Kenis, Commucke, Matanchan, Wess (aka Nepinam), Macossak, Wrutherna, Kockuinek, Winnepawin, Wenawis, and Coa, for land to the east and west of the Connecticut River that would be known as Springfield, MA. The tribesmen were paid in wampum, coats, hatchets, hoes, and knives for the land. The deed permitted the Native Americans to harvest crops they had planted, and to gather foraged food, hunt deer, and fish. Note the Native American signature marks. (Public domain)

During the morning of October 5, the Native Americans surrounded the town, but did not attack the three garrison houses. When two colonists came out to take stock of the situation, they were soon ambushed and killed by the Native Americans, who were already moving in on the fortified houses. The warriors then attacked the latter, but were repulsed by the defenders' heavy fire. They also set fire to many of Springfield's unoccupied structures, destroying a total of 32 houses and 25 barns. Just as it seemed that the three garrison houses would also be burnt to the ground, Major Robert Treat appeared on the west bank of the Connecticut River at the head of reinforcements. The intense musket fire of the natives, however, prevented Treat's militiamen from crossing the river, but their arrival did draw the attention of many of the warriors and saved the three garrison houses from imminent destruction. By the time Springfield's militiamen returned to their hometown early that afternoon, the Native Americans had already withdrawn.

The Siege of Springfield had dealt another blow to the colonists: large quantities of provisions had been lost, most of the houses in the town center had been destroyed, and the whole population was filled with terror. Springfield, however, was not abandoned, and the defenses of the town were reinforced in view of possible future assaults. The town would not be attacked again though.

The next target for King Philip's warriors was Hatfield, located on the west bank of the Connecticut River, facing Hadley on its east bank. In 1675, Hatfield was inhabited by 350 settlers, who lived in fewer than 50 houses. After the Siege of Springfield, Major Samuel Appleton had been named commander of all the militia forces stationed in the lower Connecticut River Valley, and was thus tasked with defending three main settlements: Northampton, Hatfield, and Hadley.

On October 19, 1675, a scouting party of ten militiamen marched out from Hatfield in order to gather information on the Native Americans' intentions. However, the scouts were ambushed within two miles by a band of warriors, and only one of them managed to escape; of the others, six were killed and three were taken prisoner.

The militiamen garrisoned at Hatfield sent requests for help to Northampton and Hadley. Before the Native Americans could launch their attack, reinforcements had already reached Hatfield, with Appleton taking charge of the defences. For the first time in the war, the colonists were able to repulse a Native American attack against one of their settlements. The intense fighting at Hatfield inflicted heavy losses on the attackers. This unexpected victory was the first military success for the colonists during King Philip's War, and was an extremely important morale booster. After months of setbacks and defeats, events had shown that the militiamen could repulse a Native American attack if all necessary military preparations were made.

After the attack on Hatfield, Metacomet's warriors retreated to their winter quarters and the intensity of their attacks declined. King Philip planned a great offensive the following spring, and would use the winter months to forge new alliances with other tribes.

THE GREAT SWAMP FIGHT

By the end of October 1675, the colonists had suffered a series of defeats, but had managed to defend a settlement, as the events of Hatfield had shown. Concerns remained about the possibility of the Narragansetts contributing substantial numbers of warriors to Metacomet's forces. The Narragansett tribe, the most numerous in New England, could field up to 1,000 warriors. Although the Narragansetts had launched a raid against Providence in Rhode Island, they had since professed to be neutral.

To deal with the formidable Narragansett threat, the New England colonies revived their alliance. On November 2, 1675, the New England leaders met in Boston to plan a joint operation. The colonists had learned that Canonchet, the Narragansett sachem, was assembling most of his forces in a place known as the Great Swamp, located near present-day South Kingstown, RI. Moreover, the warrior chief had begun fortifying the Great Swamp Camp, in order to protect his food stocks. The New England leaders decided that a combined force of Massachusetts, Plymouth, and Connecticut (which since 1664 had included New Haven) militiamen, joined by Mohegan warriors, would launch a surprise attack on the Great Swamp Camp.

At the beginning of December 1675, militiamen drawn from every corner of New England began to assemble into a unified force totaling some 1,150 men; 1,000 of these were colonial militiamen, while the remaining 150 were Mohegan warriors. The colonial force was organized into three regiments, according to their provenance: one for Plymouth Colony, one for Massachusetts Colony, and one for Connecticut Colony. Overall command of the force was given to Josiah Winslow, Governor of Plymouth Colony. Massachusetts contributed the highest number of militiamen: 527 in total, most of them veteran soldiers. Plymouth Colony sent just two companies totaling 159 militiamen. Connecticut deployed 300 experienced militiamen (including a company of Pequot allies) plus 150 Mohegan loyalists.

The garrison house of Richard Smith, Jr., also known as Smith's Castle, located at Wickford, RI, was chosen as the main base of operations for the Army of the United Colonies. While New England troops were assembling at Wickford, several local Native Americans were captured by the colonists,

A statue erected in Springfield to honor Miles Morgan (1616–99), a Welsh colonist who played a leading role in protecting the residents of Springfield in October 1675. His stronghouse provided shelter, and he sent a servant to contact troops in Hadley, who came to Springfield's aide. The statue, completed in 1882, is by Jonathan Scott Hartley. (Wikimedia Commons/Daderot; public domain)

Smith's Castle as it looks today, in Wickford, RI. The original fortified house of Richard Smith, built around 1640, was used by the colonists as their main advance base during the operations that led to the Great Swamp Fight. Some time after the battle, the Narragansetts destroyed the original building before raiding Providence. Smith's Castle was rebuilt by Richard Smith, Jr., in 1678, retaining some of the main features of the previous garrison house. (Wikimedia Commons/Mlanni98, CC BY-SA 4.0)

A 19th-century recreation of the colonist attack on the main entrance to the Great Swamp camp. This was heavily defended by the best native warriors, who forced back the attacking forces into the surrounding swamp. (Public domain)

including one named Peter, who soon started to collaborate with them. Among the key information he provided to them was the locations of two small Narragansett villages in the area around Wickford, which were subsequently attacked and destroyed.

Peter would act as the colonists' lead guide during their advance toward the Narragensett Great Swamp fortified camp. This camp had been built under Canonchet's direction, and was well defended. It consisted of a large village built on four to five acres of raised ground, with a stockade around

it, and was protected by an extensive swamp surrounding the camp on lower terrain. The stockade was made of thick wooden stakes fixed into the ground, reinforced with earth and brush. The camp was home to at least 500 houses and was overflowing with Wampanoag and Nipmuc refugees who sought shelter within it.

On December 15, the Narragansetts attacked a small colonist outpost located nine miles south of Wickford known as Jireh Bull's Garrison House. Fifteen colonists were killed in the attack. Three days later, the main United Colonies force moved to this outpost and set up camp for the night. In the early morning of December 19, in freezing temperatures, the Army of the United Colonies began its march toward the Great Swamp through the snow. Some time after noon that

day, the vanguard of the colonial army encountered an advance party of Narragansett warriors, and a brief skirmish ensued. At this point, the colonists discovered that the Great Swamp, which was impassable for most of the year, was frozen solid and would enable them to advance directly on the camp. The main entrance to the camp was along the trunk of a fallen tree spanning a water-filled ditch; this narrow path would present many difficulties for the colonists. Peter, however, was able to reveal that a small section of the external stockade was still unfinished, and the colonists decided to attack this point.

When the attack began, the militiamen struggled to overcome the Native American resistance: the Narragansetts delivered a devastating fire on them, and two colonial captains were shot dead. After suffering significant losses, the militiamen were pushed back towards the lower frozen swamp terrain. A second advance by the colonists, however, was much more successful: the militiamen breached the native stockade and fighting spilled into the camp. The Narragansetts fought with enormous courage to defend their homes and families, but gradually the colonists gained the upper hand thanks to their superior numbers.

Governor Winslow gave the order to set the native houses on fire, spreading panic among the civilians massed in the village. Hundreds of warriors, women, and children were killed by the militiamen or consumed by the flames that spread through their houses. All the winter stores of the Narragansett tribe were burned or spoiled, and about 100 native warriors were killed. The surviving Native Americans escaped into the frozen Great Swamp, where hundreds of them died during the following days from wounds or a lack of food and shelter. In total, around 700 Native American non-combatants died during the Great Swamp fight and in its aftermath; a further 300 Narragansetts were captured by the colonial militia.

Most of the militiamen who died during the Great Swamp Fight were buried near Smith's Castle, where the colonists had halted before launching their attack on the camp. This simple inscription commemorates the colonial casualties. (Wikimedia Commons/Mlanni98, CC BY-SA 4.0)

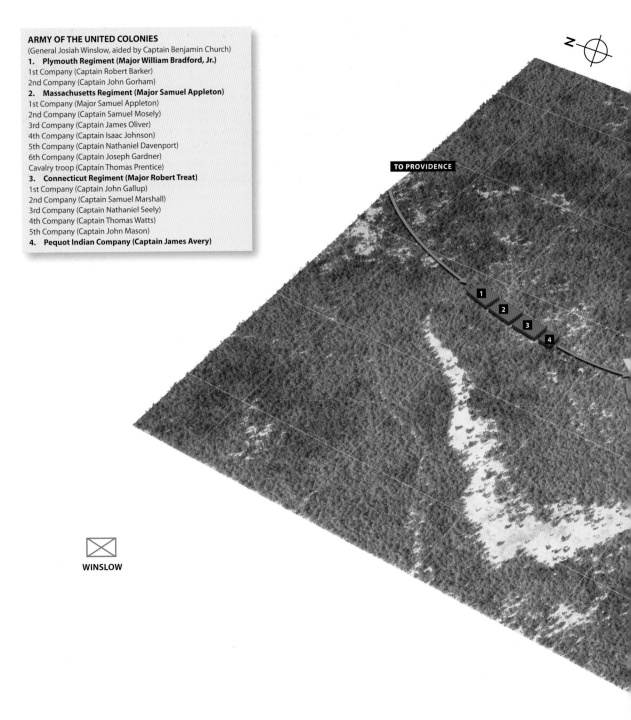

ARMY OF THE UNITED COLONIES
(General Josiah Winslow, aided by Captain Benjamin Church)

1. Plymouth Regiment (Major William Bradford, Jr.)
1st Company (Captain Robert Barker)
2nd Company (Captain John Gorham)

2. Massachusetts Regiment (Major Samuel Appleton)
1st Company (Major Samuel Appleton)
2nd Company (Captain Samuel Mosely)
3rd Company (Captain James Oliver)
4th Company (Captain Isaac Johnson)
5th Company (Captain Nathaniel Davenport)
6th Company (Captain Joseph Gardner)
Cavalry troop (Captain Thomas Prentice)

3. Connecticut Regiment (Major Robert Treat)
1st Company (Captain John Gallup)
2nd Company (Captain Samuel Marshall)
3rd Company (Captain Nathaniel Seely)
4th Company (Captain Thomas Watts)
5th Company (Captain John Mason)

4. Pequot Indian Company (Captain James Avery)

TO PROVIDENCE

WINSLOW

▼ EVENTS

1. Having marched for several hours in extremely cold temperatures and over snow-covered terrain, the Army of the United Colonies reaches the external stockade of the Narragansett camp. The colonists are guided by a renegade Native American who knows the camp well.

2. The colonial militiamen launch their attack against the camp stockade, but their first assault is repulsed with heavy losses.

3. On the advice of their Native American guide, the colonists switch their attack to an incomplete section of the enemy stockade. Using their superior numbers, the militiamen are finally able to break into the camp.

4. The colonial militiamen are ordered to destroy all the houses and food supplies inside the camp. Many non-combatants are killed by the colonists or by the fires that rage through their huts. Approximately 100 Native American warriors are killed.

5. The surviving warriors and their families flee into the frozen swamps to the south of the camp, in search of safety. Many of them will die from the extreme cold and lack of shelter. In total, more than 1,000 Native Americans will lose their lives as a result of the Great Swamp Fight.

THE GREAT SWAMP FIGHT, DECEMBER 19, 1675

At the beginning of December 1675, the colonists assembled a large army of 1,150 men with the objective of destroying the Narragansett camp built on what was known as the Great Swamp. The colonist forces included 527 Massachusetts militiamen, 300 Connecticut militiamen (with some Pequot allies), 159 Plymouth militiamen, and 150 Mohegan allied warriors. The native camp was built on four to five acres of higher ground, which was surrounded by a large swamp. The higher ground was enclosed by a stockade of thick wooden stakes fixed into the ground, reinforced with earth and brush. The camp comprised at least 500 houses, and was crowded with a large number of Native Americans seeking shelter.

GREAT SWAMP CAMP

WORDENS POND

4

A

3

5

CANONCHET

Note: gridlines are shown at intervals of 1km (0.62 miles)

NATIVE AMERICAN
A. 500–750 warriors (under Canonchet)

THE GREAT SWAMP FIGHT, DECEMBER 19, 1675 (PP. 70–71)

The Great Swamp Fight took place in bitter winter conditions. The colonial militia under Governor Josiah Winslow of Plymouth were led to the massive Narragansett settlement in South Kingstown, RI by a native guide called Indian Peter. The camp was built on 4–5 acres of raised ground, surrounded by a vast swamp and enclosed by a stockade of thick wooden stakes set into the ground (**1**). The camp comprised at least 500 dwellings and was overcrowded with Wampanoag and Nipmuc refugees.

Increase Mather records: "The English soldiers (**2**) played the men wonderfully; the Indians (**3**) also fought stoutly, but were at last beat out of their fort, which was taken by the English. There were hundreds of wigwams within the fort, which our soudiers set on fire, in the which men, women and children (no man knoweth how many hundreds of them) were burnt to death." The slaughter continued until evening, at which point the colonists withdrew.

Regarding the number of Indians killed in the Great Swamp Fight, Mather states: "the next day they found three hundred of their fighting men dead in their fort, and that many men, women and children were burned in their wigwams, but they neither knew, nor could conjecture how many: it is supposed that not less then a thousand Indian souls perished at that time." Colonist casualties were put at around 230, 85 of whom were killed including six captains (Johnson of Roxbury, Gardner of Salem, Davenport of Boston, Gallop of New London, Marshal of Windsor, and Seily of Stratford).

That night, as the colonists withdrew, "a great snow fell, also part of the army missed their way, among whom was the general himself [Winslow] with his life-guard. Had the enemy known their advantage, and pursued our soudiers … when upon their retreat, they might easily have cut off the whole army."

The effect of the fight on Native American morale was huge: "The next day the Indians finding but few English men dead in the fort amongst their three hundred Indians that were slain, were much troubled and amazed … this blow did greatly astonish them."

The Army of the United Provinces had suffered 220 casualties (70 killed and 150 wounded), not including those suffered by its Mohegan allies. The latter fought with great distinction during the battle, under the command of their war chief Oneko; these warriors had already fought King Philip at the Battle of Nipsachuc. The Great Swamp Fight was not only the largest and bloodiest battle of the war, but also a turning point in the conflict: the Narragansetts no longer represented a serious threat to the colonists, who could now focus their efforts on Metacomet and his warriors.

This simple monument, erected in 1908, commemorates the Great Swamp Fight, which today is part of a wildlife reservation. (Wikimedia Commons/Louiseannb1, CC BY-SA 4.0)

THE INTERVENTION OF THE MOHAWKS

After the Great Swamp Fight, Metacomet and his Wampanoag and Pocumtuc warriors moved northwest to a camp in Mahican territory, at what is now Hoosick, NY. There, he hoped, his men could continue the war from a base beyond the boundaries of the New England colonies. They also might recruit Mahican warriors to join them, or perhaps even Mohawks.

During the winter of 1675/76, hundreds of starving fugitives from New England were drawn to Metacomet's camp. The neighboring Mahicans tried to aid them, but they were no longer a numerous people. In 1669, the Mahicans, joined by the Pocumtuc tribes and several other New England nations, had attacked the Mohawks. The Mohawks, reinforced by other Iroquois warriors, then destroyed the Mahicans. By 1772, the 1,000 surviving Mahicans had been reduced to a subject people.

When news of Metacomet's camp reached the Mohawks and New York governor Edmund Andros, who cared little about the fate of the New England settlers, Andros urged the Mohawks to order the intruders either to submit to the Iroquois and end their war, or leave the territory of the Mahicans. Metacomet refused to submit to the Iroquois, but agreed to leave. His people then moved east to a camp in Pocumtuc territory, in what is now Northfield, MA. Some of his angry warriors, however, left behind several dead Mohawks.

During late February 1676, the enraged Mohawks attacked Metacomet's new camp. The ensuing battle, which took place in woodland terrain and in very cold temperatures, pitted King Philip's 900 warriors against a similarly sized force of Mohawks. Little is recorded of this clash, in which Metacomet's men were taken by surprise, but by the end, over 400 of King Philip's warriors had been killed or captured. It represented King Philip's worst defeat of the war, and, alongside the Great Swamp Fight, was one of the most decisive battles of the conflict. Although Metacomet was once again able to escape capture, this clash with the Mohawks signaled the beginning of the end for him. More than half of the warriors that he had assembled over the previous months were lost, and the survivors returned to New England.

Mohawk raiders then pursued the New England fugitives through the rest of the year. As Metacomet's warriors resumed their raids against the colonists, Mohawk raiders threatened the villages of his warriors. A rescued English captive told Increase Mather "that the Indians where he was would not suffer any fires to be made in the night, for fear lest the Mohawks should thereby discern where they were and cut them off."

THE LANCASTER RAID AND THE ATTACK ON MEDFIELD

On February 10, 1676, a band of Nipmuc warriors (allied to King Philip) led by the chief Monoco attacked the settlement of Lancaster in Massachusetts.

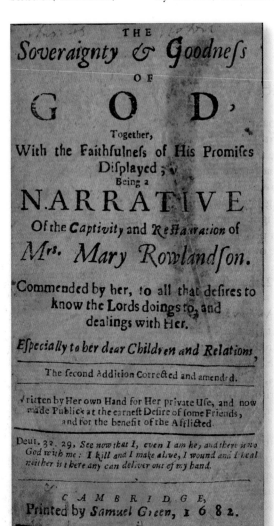

The soveraignty & goodness of God: together, with the faithfulness of his promises displayed: being a narrative of the captivity and restauration of Mrs. Mary Rowlandson, published in 1682. Mary was captured at Lancaster on February 10, 1675, by Native American raiders led by Monoco, and held for nearly 12 weeks before being ransomed. Her narrative became a bestseller. (Public domain)

Lancaster was a typical settlement, populated by 50 homesteads clustered around six garrison houses. The latter had been constructed after an earlier Nipmuc attack on the town in August 1675, in which several inhabitants were killed. The settlement had a small garrison of 15 militiamen, too few in number to protect it from a Native American attack involving hundreds of warriors. The colonists did, however, have some forewarning that an attack might be imminent, from two Native American spies who passed them information in late January; the colonial authorities, however, largely ignored this and failed to reinforce the garrison in time.

The Narragansett, Nipmuc, and Wampanoag warriors (led by Monoco) attacked Lancaster on February 10, 1676, first burning the bridge over the river to prevent any reinforcements from reaching the town. The houses and barns were set alight, and the garrison house of Reverend Joseph Rowlandson, who was absent in Boston attempting to organize reinforcements for the settlement, was also set ablaze. Its defenders were forced to leave the garrison house to save themselves; some were killed, while others were captured, including several injured women and children, among them Mary Rowlandson, wife of Reverend Rowlandson. Mary would later write a popular narrative of her captivity.

Before the Native American warriors could destroy the other garrison houses, 40 militiamen led by Captain Samuel Wadsworth arrived at Lancaster from the east. Monoco's men ceased their assault as soon as Wadsworth's force arrived, but before abandoning Lancaster, they made sure its buildings

The site of the raid on Lancaster as it looks today. The landscape has changed little since King Philip's War. (Photo courtesy of Eric B. Schultz)

were destroyed and carried off any food supplies they could find. The Lancaster Raid resulted in the deaths of 50 of its inhabitants, while another 24 (mostly women and children) were carried off as prisoners. On March 26, 1676, Lancaster was abandoned and its surviving inhabitants relocated to nearby settlements.

The settlement of Medfield, with a population of aroud 250 souls, felt particularly exposed to Native American attack in the wake of recent events. Located just a few miles southeast of Lancaster, its inhabitants soon heard the terrifying news from the latter settlement. On February 14, the town's Reverend Wilson wrote to Massachusett's governor Leverett asking for reinforcements to be dispatched to bolster the town's defenses. The Massachusetts Bay's colonial authorities responded immediately and dispatched 80 foot soldiers and 20 cavalry troopers to the town. The foot soldiers were commanded by Captain John Jacob, while the mounted ones were under the orders of Captain Edward Oaks. A further 25 men under Captain Gibbs of Watertown also arrived to help. The militia captains understood that Medfield was likely Monoco's next target, and

The site of the garrison house (since lost) of Reverend Joseph Rowlandson at Lancaster. The tree marks the location. It was from here that Mary Rowlandson, wife of the minister, was taken into captivity. The photograph is from *King Philip's War* (1906). (Public domain)

The commemorative stone at Lancaster. (Photo courtesy of Eric B. Schultz)

thus prepared as best they could for an imminent attack. The militiamen were billeted around the settlement, which also had over 50 firearms at the disposal of its settlers.

On February 21, 1676, just before daybreak, a Native American war party again under Monoco's leadership and numbering several hundred strong, silently entered the town. As dawn broke, they struck. The terrified residents began to flee to the garrison houses to take shelter, as the Native American warriors set the town ablaze. Thirty-two of its houses, two mills, and numerous barns were destroyed by fire, and some 17 colonists were killed, men, women, and children. Medfield was located just 22 miles from Boston, which further raised concerns that the Native Americans could soon attack New England's major urban centers.

The next settlement to be targeted was Groton, which was inhabited by 60 families. Although it featured five garrison houses, it was not well supplied with ammunition and food stocks. On March 2, 1676, Groton was attacked by a small party of Native American warriors, who caused only light damage to the settlement. This led to colonist militiamen arriving in the town to protect it. On March 13, however, Monoco attacked with a war party that was 400 strong. He used the same stealth tactic employed at Medfield, with his warriors silently making their way into the settlement under cover of darkness, without alerting the colonists. At sunrise, they began their attack. The militiamen occupying one of the garrison houses went outside in an attempt to halt the Native American

The Redemption Rock, in Princeton, MA. It was here that, on May 2, 1676, Mary Rowlandson was released from captivity. Joan Hoar, a prominent lawyer and Indian missionary who was sent to negotiate with her Native American captors, paid a £20 ransom in order to free her. (Photo courtesy of Eric B. Schultz)

assault, but were soon set upon and killed. The troops in the remaining four garrison houses, however, gave resistance from their positions. The Native Americans destroyed many of the town's buildings, including the meeting house and 40 homes. That evening, the Native Americans left the settlement and went back to their main base at Menameset. Groton's surviving inhabitants soon abandoned the settlement and made for Concord. A further misfortune awaited the survivors en route, as they were struck by a Native American ambush. Most managed to escape and make it to safety, however. Groton would not be repopulated for another two years.

The attack on Groton is emblematic of the military actions that took place during this phase of King Philip's War. Once a settlement had been destroyed, save for its garrison houses, the surviving inhabitants would abandon their settlement and move towards a larger, safer place. It was becoming clear that many of the more remote colonial settlements would soon be abandoned, with settlement confined to a few major centers located on or near to the coast. Even then, the future of these larger centers, like Boston or Plymouth, appeared uncertain.

THE ATTACKS ON NORTHAMPTON AND MARLBOROUGH

Northampton in Massachusetts was one of the few major colonial settlements of the New England frontier areas yet to be attacked by Native Americans. It was inhabited by around 500 people, and had been recently fortified with the construction of a wooden stockade that enclosed most of its structures. After the previous Native American raids that had ravaged nearby settlements, Northampton was heavily garrisoned by 300 militiamen in three companies: one from Massachusetts Colony under command of Captain William Turner, and two from Connecticut Colony under command of Major Robert Treat. Up until the beginning of March 1676, Northampton had not been garrisoned, and thus could have presented an easy target for King Philip's warriors; between March 8 and 13, however, Turner and Treat arrived in the settlement with their forces.

The early seal of Plymouth Colony, created in 1629. The four (apparently Native American) figures each carry the symbolic burning heart of John Calvin. (Public domain)

On the morning of March 14, a sizeable force of Native American warriors, including experienced Nipmuc and Narragansett fighters, assaulted Northampton. They were soon able to break through the stockade at three different points, and then targeted the houses. One of the latter was set on fire before the militiamen mustered a counter-attack, which killed or injured several of the Native Americans. The latter found themselves facing a trap within the stockade, and having realized that a large militia force was present in the town, the warriors decided to halt their attack and withdrew outside the settlement. Four colonist men and one woman were killed in the raid, and several houses and barns outside the stockade were burned down. Major damage, however, was averted. The defense of Northampton proved to be a significant victory for the colonists, having preserved one of their major frontier settlements.

In 1676, Marlborough was a small town inhabited by just over 200 settlers living in 30 dwellings. Although modest in size, it occupied a strategic location on the Connecticut Road that connected Boston to the Connecticut River Valley settlements, and had eight garrison houses. The town also featured a small stone fort. A company of militiamen was present in the town, under the command of Captain Samuel Brocklebank, who was in charge of the town's defenses but not present at the time of the attack on the settlement.

On Sunday, March 26, the Native Americans attacked Marlborough, and "consumed a great part of the town" as Increase Mather records. The attack took place while most of the inhabitants were assembled in the meeting house to hear a sermon by the Reverend Brimsmead. A cry arose from outside of "The Indians are upon us!" causing panic and terror among the inhabitants, who began to flee for the shelter of the town's garrison houses.

The Native American attack was violent and rapid; 24 houses and barns were destroyed in Marlborough, most of the food stocks were taken, and a large number of cattle were killed, maimed, or driven away. The meeting house was also destroyed by fire. That evening, the colonist militiamen, led by Lieutenant Jacob, managed to organize a counter-attack on the Native Americans encamped outside the settlement, killing or wounding around 40 of them according to Jacob. The Native Americans then withdrew.

PIERCE'S FIGHT

After the Great Swamp Fight, Narragansett warriors had remained active in Rhode Island, but the losses suffered in December 1675 meant they were too few to launch large-scale raids against the more sizeable colonial settlements.

In March 1676, the colonists learned that a substantial group of Narragansett warriors was assembling at Pawtucket Falls, probably with the intention of building a new camp there. In order to prevent the Native Americans establishing a new base in this area, Captain Michael Pierce of Scituate, MA, assembled a force of around 50 militiamen and 20 allied Native Americans, and marched against the Pawtucket camp. Pierce's militiamen had been assembled from a variety of New England settlements, including Scituate, Marshfield, Duxbury, Sandwich, Barnstable, Yarmouth, and Eastham.

On March 25, 1676, while still en route, the colonists were attacked by a small group of Narragansett warriors. In the ensuing skirmish, the colonists killed several Native Americans, for no loss to their own men. The Narragansetts had apparently sent this smaller group of warriors to probe the strength, and fighting resolve, of the colonist column.

Despite his initial success at fighting off the warriors, Pierce was concerned that the Native Americans would return to attack his men that night; given that his advance had been slowed by the assault, his men would now be unable to reach Pawtucket Falls before darkness fell. Thus, Pierce ordered a retreat back to the garrison house at Old Rehoboth, where his men spent the night. There they received intelligence that the Native Americans were gathering at a site near the Blackstone River.

The following day, the militiamen resumed their march, stalked by Native American scouts observing their movements. At a certain point, while they were close to a fording spot on the Blackstone River, near the house of William Blackstone, the militiamen spotted a small band of Narragansett warriors fleeing; but this was a cunning ruse, to induce them to follow the Native Americans in pursuit—for "they went limping to make the English believe they were lame, till they had led them into a snare," as Increase Mather records. Captain Pierce allowed his men to follow the retreating warriors into the nearby woods. Here, 500 Narragansett, Wampanoag, Nashaway, Nipmuc, and Podunk warriors were waiting in ambush for the militiamen, and as soon as the latter entered the forest, the Native Americans sprang their trap. The Native Americans had also staged a party of warriors on the opposite riverbank, to prevent Pierce's men from crossing the river to safety. They were to all intents and purposes surrounded, and attacks began to hit them from all sides.

The fighting continued for two hours, with Pierce deploying his men in a defensive circle, but the Native Americans (who were possibly under the command of the chief Narragansett sachem Canonchet) were present in overwhelming numbers, pointing to only one, inevitable outcome: certain death for the colonists. Some 50 or so militiamen, including Pierce himself, were killed, together with eight to ten Native American allies. "How many of the enemy fell," records Increase Mather, "we know not certainly, only we hear that some Indians, which have since been taken by the English, confess that Captain Pierce, and those with him killed an hundred and forty of them before they lost their own lives." Nine militiamen managed to escape, but were later captured and subsequently tortured and executed near Cumberland, RI. Their mutilated bodies were later discovered and buried by colonial militiamen. Pierce's Fight (also known as Nine Men's Misery) had been a disaster for the colonists. A cairn still marks the site today of where the nine men met their gruesome deaths. When news reached Rehoboth of the predicament of Pierce and his men, a militia company was dispatched to come to his aid; but they only arrived in time to administer the last rites to the dying and to give the dignity of burial to their dead.

FURTHER ATTACKS, MARCH–APRIL 1676

The settlement of Sudbury, located on the east side of the Sudbury River, provided a further target for King Philip's warriors, who needed to constantly regenerate their supplies of food, ammunition, and weapons to continue their war. Most of Sudbury's garrison houses and its mills were located on the west side of the Sudbury River. A wooden bridge connected the largest part of the settlement with the houses on the other bank.

On March 27, the inhabitants of Sudbury, having heard of the recent fate of Marlborough, decided not to merely await the inevitable, as Increase Mather records:

The colonist Edmund Rice built this house *c*. 1643 in saltbox style (with a long, pitched roof sloping down to the back), by a spring to the east of the Sudbury River (Old Connecticut Path, Wayland, MA). It burned down sometime around 1910. At the time of Rice's death in May 1663, his large estates were valued at over £740—a considerable sum. (Wikimedia Commons; public domain)

Some of the inhabitants of Sudbury, being alarumed by what the Indians did yesterday to their neighbours in Malbury [Marlborough], apprehending they might come upon the enemy unawares, in case they should march after them in the night time, they resolved to try what might be done, and that not altogether without success. For towards the morning whilst it was yet dark, they discerned where the Indians lay by their fires. And such was their boldness, as that about three hundred of them lay all night, within half a mile of one of the garison houses in that town … Albeit the darkness was such as an English man could not be discerned from an Indian, yet ours being forty in number, discharged several times upon the enemy, and (as Indians taken since that time do confess,) God so disposed of the bullets that were shot at that time, that no less then thirty Indians were wounded, of whom there were fourteen that dyed, several of which had been principal actors in the late bloudy tragedyes. They fired hard upon the English, but neither killed nor wounded so much as one man in the skirmish.

On March 28, 1676, the Native Americans attacked the settlement of Old Rehoboth. Mather records that the "Indians burnt about thirty barns, and near upon fourty dwelling houses in Rehoboth, so that thereby the dissipation and desolation of that Church is greatly threatned."

The town of Providence, RI —the most important conurbation in Rhode Island, although still a modest farming and fishing town, located along the eastern shore of the Providence River—was home to 500 settlers at the time of the outbreak of the war. However, the fear of Native American attacks had seen its population shrink down to fewer than 50 souls. On March 29, 1676, Canonchet attacked it and destroyed 54 of its houses, forcing the few surviving settlers to abandon it. Further minor incidents and alarms also took place at Chelmsford, Andover, Cambridge, Weymouth, and Billerica.

THE CAPTURE OF CANONCHET

On April 3, 1676, in order to halt the Narragansett raids against Rhode Island settlements, Captain George Denison of the Connecticut militia advanced on Pawtucket at the head of a military force comprising 50 militiamen and 80 allied Native Americans (Niantics, Pequots, and Mohegans). Denison was informed by a captured Narragansett woman that Canonchet's camp was not far from his position; the warrior chief, in fact, had temporarily returned to his home with just 30 warriors in order to seek seed corn for the ongoing spring planting. The Native Americans also needed to produce their food supplies to see them through the following winter, and thus could not abandon their own plantations. The colonists saw a great opportunity to eliminate the dangerous warrior chief while accompanied by only a small warrior band.

Canonchet was not expecting an attack by the colonists and thus had not taken any precautions to defend his camp. The militiamen were able to approach the camp without being noticed, and caught the Native Americans by surprise. The Narragansetts were massacred within the space of a few minutes, and few escaped from the camp, which was built on a hill. Canonchet made for the reverse side of the hill, discarding his cloak, silver-trimmed coat, and wampum belt in order to run more speedily; but he was soon encircled and had no choice but to surrender.

Canonchet was then taken to Connecticut, where he was offered his life in return for an end to the Narragansetts' raids. The great warrior chief, son of Miantonomo, refused to submit. When informed that he was to be executed, he is reported to have said: "I like it well. I shall die before my heart is soft, and before I have spoken a word unworthy of myself." The death sentence was carried out by the Mohegan sachem Oneko, a Pequot warrior called Robin Cassacinamon, and the Niantic sachem Harman Garrett, at Stonington,

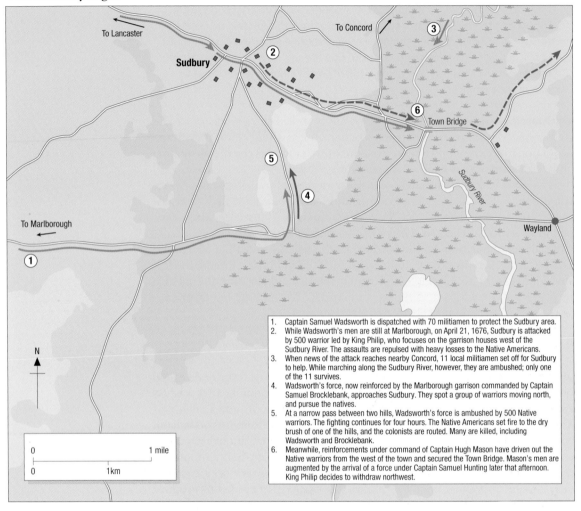

1. Captain Samuel Wadsworth is dispatched with 70 militiamen to protect the Sudbury area.
2. While Wadsworth's men are still at Marlborough, on April 21, 1676, Sudbury is attacked by 500 warrior led by King Philip, who focuses on the garrison houses west of the Sudbury River. The assaults are repulsed with heavy losses to the Native Americans.
3. When news of the attack reaches nearby Concord, 11 local militiamen set off for Sudbury to help. While marching along the Sudbury River, however, they are ambushed; only one of the 11 survives.
4. Wadsworth's force, now reinforced by the Marlborough garrison commanded by Captain Samuel Brocklebank, approaches Sudbury. They spot a group of warriors moving north, and pursue the natives.
5. At a narrow pass between two hills, Wadsworth's force is ambushed by 500 Native warriors. The fighting continues for four hours. The Native Americans set fire to the dry brush of one of the hills, and the colonists are routed. Many are killed, including Wadsworth and Brocklebank.
6. Meanwhile, reinforcements under command of Captain Hugh Mason have driven out the Native warriors from the west of the town and secured the Town Bridge. Mason's men are augmented by the arrival of a force under Captain Samuel Hunting later that afternoon. King Philip decides to withdraw northwest.

CT. His severed head was taken to Hartford, as a warning sign to any rebel sachems that the colonial authorities would give them no quarter.

On April 20, 19 houses and barns were burned down by Native American warriors at Scituate in Plymouth Colony. Further destruced was avoided by the stiff resistance of the settlement's inhabitants.

THE SUDBURY FIGHT

The colonial authorities were also taking action to protect the Sudbury settlement. Captain Samuel Wadsworth and 70 militiamen had been dispatched to the town to reinforce its garrison, but the settlement would come under concerted attack before they could arrive.

The Native Americans had opted to target Sudbury over Concord. Mary Rowlandson, who was being held captive in the Mount Wachusett camp, located some 25 miles northwest of Sudbury near modern Princeton, recalls the moment the decision was taken to attack Sudbury:

Before they went to that fight they got a company together to pow-wow. The manner was as followeth: there was one that kneeled upon a deerskin, with the company round him in a ring who kneeled, and striking upon the ground with their hands, and with sticks, and muttering or humming with their mouths … Then he on the deerskin made a speech, and all manifested assent to it; and so they did many times together … And then he upon the deerskin, made another speech unto which they all assented in a rejoicing manner. And so they ended their business, and forthwith went to Sudbury fight.

The attack on Sudbury was carried out by around 500 Native American warriors, under Muttawmp's command. The attackers opted to concentrate their forces on the garrison houses located west of the Sudbury River, perhaps tempted by their stores of food, water, weapons, and ammunition. Despite all their efforts, the Native Americans were unable to take the garrison houses, and their assaults were repulsed with heavy losses. Metacomet's warriors tried to destroy one of the garrison houses by using a cart they had set on fire, but when this was pushed toward the fortified building, one of its wheels struck a rock and the cart fell apart. The now-lost Haynes Garrison House on Water Row Road (north of the modern Old Sudbury Road, Route 27) saw particularly heavy exchanges of fire.

Coordinating the defense of Sudbury was the town's chief of militia, John Grout, who had moved to Sudbury in 1663, and was one of its leading citizens. Grout was around 60 years of age, and together with his militiamen (which numbered around 80 strong), managed to hold off the Native American attackers for around three hours, until vital reinforcements arrived—for without them, the settlers would inevitably succumb over time. The settlers to the east of the river had fled to safety of a stockade some distance to the south; the destruction on this side appears to have been much less than to the settlement to the west.

When news of the attack against Sudbury reached the nearby settlement of Concord, 11 militiamen set off to come to its aid and bring help to the local inhabitants. While marching along the Sudbury River, however, they were ambushed by Native Americans, near to the location of the Haynes Garrison House; only one of the 11 colonists survived. In the early afternoon, reinforcements under the command of Captain Hugh Mason reached Sudbury and drove off the Native Americans from the west side of the settlement, retaking the wooden bridge that crossed the river.

While these events were taking place in Sudbury, Captain Wadsworth in Marlborough was informed of the Native American attack. He and his exhausted militiamen were heading northwest toward the town some ten miles distant, reinforced by Marlborough's original garrison under Captain Samuel Brocklebank. While approaching Sudbury, the militiamen noticed a group of warriors moving northward; thinking that these were the rear-guard of the war party that had just attacked Sudbury retreating back, they pursued the Native Americans, hoping to catch up with King Philip's main body of warriors. When the militiamen reached a narrow pass between two hills (today located between Greenhill Road and Goodman's Hill Road), however, they were ambushed by a large party of 500 Native Americans, who were probably moving toward Sudbury in support of Metacomet's attack. This time, however, the militiamen rapidly formed a defensive position at the top of Greenhill, and

The location of the Sudbury Fight, taken from *King Philip's War* (1906). (Public domain)

were able to repulse several attacks while holding their position.

After several hours of fighting, the Native Americans withdrew. With the sun going down, the colonists hoped to escape from their position without being attacked. It was at this point, however, that the Native Americans set the dry brush of the hill on fire, seeking to force the colonists to flee from the flames and smoke, downhill toward the southwest. Some took refuge in a mill building there, while others were killed or captured. Wadsworth and Brocklebank were both slain. Those in the mill were rescued later by reinforcements.

In Sudbury, Mason's men were bolstered by the arrival of Captain Samuel Hunting with his allied Native American troops. Once the reinforcements reached the settlement, King Philip chose to withdraw east of the Sudbury River, heading back to his base near Mount Wachusett. Although his warriors had not been able to destroy Sudbury, they had ambushed and killed a large number of colonists; but they too had lost warriors, and failed to secure the food and weaponry from the stronghouses. Mary Rowlandson records their return to camp after the Sudbury Fight:

> For they said they had killed two captains and almost an hundred men. One Englishman they brought along with them: and he said, it was too true, for they had made sad work at Sudbury, as indeed it proved. Yet they came home without that rejoicing and triumphing over their victory which they were wont to show at other times; but rather like dogs (as they say) which have lost their ears.

Increase Mather claims that any captured Sudbury colonists or militiamen were subsequently tortured and killed:

> [They] took five or six of the English and carried them away alive, but that night killed them in such a manner as none but salvages would have done. For they stripped them naked, and caused them to run the gauntlet, whipping them after a cruel and bloudy manner, and then threw hot ashes upon them; cut out the flesh of their legs, and put fire into their wounds, delighting to see the miserable torments of wretched creatures.

THE BATTLE OF TURNER'S FALLS

On May 8, 17 houses and barns were set on fire at Bridgewater, also in Plymouth Colony, and four colonist men were murdered at Taunton whilst working in their fields. Only a heavy downpour prevented further deaths, causing the Native American warriors to call off their assault. By this time, many of Metacomet's warriors were focused on the planting of crops, and

Turner's Falls

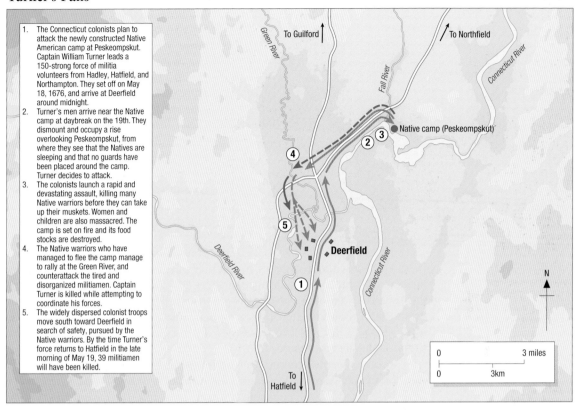

1. The Connecticut colonists plan to attack the newly constructed Native American camp at Peskeompskut. Captain William Turner leads a 150-strong force of militia volunteers from Hadley, Hatfield, and Northampton. They set off on May 18, 1676, and arrive at Deerfield around midnight.
2. Turner's men arrive near the Native camp at daybreak on the 19th. They dismount and occupy a rise overlooking Peskeompskut, from where they see that the Natives are sleeping and that no guards have been placed around the camp. Turner decides to attack.
3. The colonists launch a rapid and devastating assault, killing many Native warriors before they can take up their muskets. Women and children are also massacred. The camp is set on fire and its food stocks are destroyed.
4. The Native warriors who have managed to flee the camp manage to rally at the Green River, and counterattack the tired and disorganized militiamen. Captain Turner is killed while attempting to coordinate his forces.
5. The widely dispersed colonist troops move south toward Deerfield in search of safety, pursued by the Native warriors. By the time Turner's force returns to Hatfield in the late morning of May 19, 39 militiamen will have been killed.

hunting for game that their families would need for food until the crops were harvested in August. The colonial capital Plymouth was also targeted, on May 11, as recorded by Increase Mather:

> A company of Indians assaulted the Town of Plimouth, burnt eleven houses and five barns therein: ten Englishmen were going to seek after the enemy, and having an Indian with them, who was true to the English, he spied a party of Indians lying in ambush, who in probability had otherwise cut off many of them, but the English having the opportunity of the first shot, struck down several Indians, one of which had on a great peag belt. But he and the other that fell were dragged away, and the Indians fled, when they saw themselves pursued, though but by a few. Nevertheless two days after this, they burnt seven houses and two barns more in Plimouth, and the remaining houses in Namasket [Middleborough].

In Connecticut, small bands of native warriors, coming from the upper Connecticut River Valley, continued to harass the local colonists and raided several outposts. The Connecticut settlers were unable to work in their plantations without running the risk of being attacked by Native American warriors. The colonists petitioned the colonial authorities to launch an action similar to that which resulted in the Great Swamp Fight; the militia forces stationed in the area, however, were limited, consisting of just 50 militiamen garrisoned in Hadley, under the command of Captain William Turner, plus another 55 men stationed in Springfield and Northampton. The Connecticut

The riverbank at Turner's Falls, down which the colonists drove the Native American warriors. The photograph is from *King Philip's War* (1906). (Public domain)

colonists were aware that the raids against their property originated from a large camp at Peskeompskut, near present-day Montague.

When a band of warriors from Peskeompskut carried off 70 horses and cattle that belonged to the settlers, Turner was forced to act. After calling for volunteers from Hadley, Hatfield, and Northampton, he was able to assemble a force of some 150 mounted militiamen. On May 18, 1676, before sundown, they set off toward Peskeompskut, which lay 20 miles to the north. Around midnight, the militiamen arrived at Deerfield, but without stopping to rest they pushed on to their target, arriving there at daybreak. Before moving against the camp, they dismounted from their horses and took up positions on a steep hill overlooking Peskeompskut. From there, they saw that the camp was quiet and the Native Americans were sleeping. Because there were no scouts placed around the camp, the colonists decided to attack.

The militiamen fell among the Native American houses and killed many of their inhabitants before the warriors could take up weapons. Increase Mather records: "our souldiers came and put their guns into their wigwams, before the Indians were aware of them, and made a great and notable slaughter amongst them." When a few surviving warriors managed to escape from the camp, the colonists continued their indiscriminate assault by massacring all the women and children they could find. The camp was set on fire and all the food reserves of the Native Americans were destroyed.

However, a sense of panic now gripped the colonist attackers, as Mather records:

> an English captive lad, who was found in the wigwams, spake as if Philip were coming with a thousand Indians: which false report being famed among the souldiers, a pannick terror fell upon many of them, and they hasted homewards in a confused rout.

The Native American warriors who had escaped, bolstered by the arrival of further warriors who had heard of the attack, gathered themselves on the west bank of the nearby Green River, reorganized, and launched a furious counter-attack against the by now exhausted and disorganized militiamen. While attempting to conduct an organized retreat for his men, Captain Turner was killed by a Native American. The scattered colonists began to withdraw south toward Deerfield, in search of safety, pursued closely by the Native Americans, who cut down all those colonists who had become separated from the main body or were too slow in their retreat.

By the time the survivors of Turner's expedition made it back to Hatfield, in the late morning of May 19, 39 of the original contingent had been killed.

A few days later, Turner's body was found a short distance from the river; he had been shot through the thigh and back, and appeared to have suffered a quick death.

After this unexpected and devastating defeat, the colonial authorities were forced to dispatch Captain Benjamin Newbury and 80 men from the Connecticut River area to defend against Native American incursions. However, the Battle of Turner's Falls had inflicted serious losses on the Native Americans of the Connecticut River Valley—200 dead, and much of their food supplies destroyed. The ability of the Connecticut Native Americans to mount a serious threat to the colonists was greatly diminished as a result.

THE ATTACK ON HADLEY

The last major clash of King Philip's War took place in June 1676 at Hadley, a settlement located on a bend of the Connecticut River, on the eastern bank, not far from Northampton. Due to its strategic and easily defensible position, Hadley had been chosen by the colonial authorities as a major base for operations against the Native American tribes. The latter comprised a joint Massachusetts–Connecticut militia pincer movement

A 19th-century depiction of King Philip's Seat at Mount Hope. (Public domain)

heading northwards on both sides of the river, to clear pro-Metacomet warriors from the terrain alongside the river, where the colonist settlements were located. Hadley was well fortified, well garrisoned, and had plentiful food reserves. The settlement was protected on three sides by the Connecticut River, and on the remaining side a long wooden stockade stretching from riverbank to riverbank had been erected. Hadley also at the time was home to 200 loyal Native Americans, who held King Philip as a common enemy.

According to Increase Mather's account of the attack on June 12, 1676, three militiamen had ventured outside the gate in the stockade unarmed that morning, but were soon seen by the sentry returning at full speed, pursued by 20 or so Native American warriors, who then hacked them down. The alarm was raised in the town, and the Connecticut militiamen present in the town and their Native American allies managed to drive the attackers away from the southern end of the settlement. However, they were then set upon by a much larger number (over 500, it seems) of Native Americans who had been lying in wait in the bushes and woods around the town. The Native American attackers then targeted the northern end of the town, setting some

King Philip's Seat as it appears today. The nearby Haffenreffer Museum of Anthropology contains various historical artefacts related to King Philip's War and to the Native Americans of New England during the 17th century. (Photo courtesy of Barrington Land Conservation Trust)

buildings alight, before the discharge of "a great gun" brought them to a halt and caused panic and slaughter among their numbers. Metacomet's warriors then pulled back, and were pursued for two miles out of town by the militiamen and loyal Native American warriors. Not wishing to extend their pursuit too far, for risk of leaving Hadley exposed, the colonist forces halted and return to the town.

Events at Hadley spawned a piece of folklore based around a character known as the "Angel of Hadley." Legend has it that, when Hadley was attacked by the Native Americans, an elderly man suddenly appeared and organized the local residents in the successful defense of their community. Some have identified this figure with the roundhead General William Goffe, who was wanted for his role in the execution of King Charles I in England, and who was known to have fled to New England. Some scholars have suggested that Increase Mather's account of the Hadley attack contains deliberate inaccuracies (including the presence of militiamen in the town at the time of the attack—records indicate they were actually moving up the Connecticut River Valley in a pincer movement along both banks), which were inserted to protect the known whereabouts of Goffe, Mather being one of those who sympathized with his plight. The legend has also been linked by some to an earlier attack on Hadley in September 1675, and not the 1676 assault.

METACOMET'S DEATH

Some of King Philip's supporters had begun to abandon his cause. They understood that his forces would never be able to take the major fortified cities of the colonists, and now, exhausted by the war and their efforts to survive, they attempted to make peace with the colonists. More than 400 Native Americans who had supported Metacomet surrendered to the colonists by early July 1676.

A 19th-century reconstruction of the death of Metacomet. Two rangers were lying in wait for the Wampanoag chief, and both opened fire. The ranger's shot missed him, but the aim of Native American John Alderman was true, and killed King Philip. (Public domain)

The greatest prize for the colonial authorities was obviously the capture or killing of Metacomet. The Wampanoag sachem had returned to Plymouth Colony territory, and was attempting to join his remaining warriors with those of the Narragansetts. If King Philip were captured or killed, the resistance of the Native Americans would rapidly collapse.

On August 9, 1676, Captain Benjamin Church departed Plymouth with his elite company of rangers on a mission to track down Metacomet. Church explored the woods around Pocasset and then crossed the narrows of the Sakonnet River in search of King Philip. Rumors had indicated that the sachem had returned to his home territory and was now moving south toward Rhode Island. On August 11, Benjamin Church received confirmation from a Wampanoag warrior who had left Metacomet's camp that the sachem was back at Mount Hope. It appears this warrior had abandoned Metacomet's cause because the latter had killed his brother, for suggesting to the sachem that he should make peace with the colonists since there was no hope of victory for the Wampanoags. Harnessing this Native American warrior's desire for revenge, Church used him as a guide on his approach toward Mount Hope.

The Wampanoag camp was located in a small area of upland terrain, at the southern end of a swamp lying at the foot of Mount Hope. Benjamin Church knew this area well and had a clear vision in his mind of where the enemy camp was located, even before seeing it.

Benjamin Church pulled Metacomet's body from the mud and ordered his rangers to remove his head and quarter his body. (Public domain)

The site of Metacomet's death. The photograph is from *King Philip's War* (1906). (Public domain)

On August 12, at daybreak, a small group of rangers (guided by Captain Roger Goulding) silently approached Metacomet's camp. Goulding, however, was spotted by one of the camp's guards, and was forced to loose off a shot with his musket. The Wampanoags were alerted by its sound and many began to make for the safety of the swamp. Metacomet, with his rifle in hand, ran as fast as he could to escape capture, pursued by the allied Native Americans under Church's command.

At a certain point, King Philip ran across two rangers (one colonist and one Native American) who were lying in wait behind a tree. The colonist fired first, but missed the sachem; the shot fire by the Native American struck Metacomet, who fell face forward in a pool of water, his gun beneath him. The Native American ranger who had killed the sachem was given the name John Alderman by the colonists.

Church had Metacomet's body pulled from the swamp, and ordered his Native American rangers to remove his head and then quarter his body—to mark his traitor's status. Metacomet's head was taken to Plymouth and set on a pole, where it remained on public display for an entire generation. The rangers who had taken part in the operation were given prize money, while John Alderman was allowed to keep one of King Philip's hands as a memento.

THE WAR IN MAINE

In 1676, French and Abenaki raiders destroyed most of the small English settlements in southern Maine. The local fishing industry, which had flourished before the war, was badly affected. The death of Metacomet, moreover, did not affect the war.

In 1678, a successful English operation ended with the capture of 150 Abenaki warriors. Peace then followed. After the deaths or capture of nearly 300 English settlers, the Treaty of Casco established an uneasy peace on the northern border of New England. Some sporadic raids, however, continued until 1679.

AFTERMATH

With the deaths of Canonchet and Metacomet, most of the Native American warriors lost their enthusiasm for the anti-colonist cause, and opted to surrender. Hundreds were captured across the whole of New England, including the warrior chiefs Muttawmp and Monoco, who were later executed for their part in the conflict.

By August 1676, New England had changed considerably. Nearly 1,000 colonists and thousands of Native Americans had died in the conflict. More than half of the New England settlements had been destroyed or attacked. The whole frontier area between the settlers and Native Americans was in a state of ruin. The colonists had lost most of what they had built up over the previous three decades, but still had adequate resources to rebuild what had been destroyed during the war. The Native American tribes, however, had seen their populations decimated, their leading warriors killed, and their tribal leaders exterminated or deposed.

For the colonists, King Philip's War reinforced the concept of uniting forces to defeat a common enemy. In London, conversely, it was becoming clearer that the North American colonies had a growing sense of military independence. A century later, the Thirteen Colonies would merge to form an independent nation, but some of the earliest seeds of this new sense of self-determination were sown in the dark days of King Philip's War.

The war also witnessed the definitive abandonment of any dreams the Native Americans had of expelling the colonists from New England. Their enemies were by now too numerous and too well organized to be defeated. The threat posed by the rebel Native American tribes of southern New England was eliminated, leading a process of absorption, physically and culturally, into the expanding colonial settlements.

The colonists also learned the crucial lesson that the only way to counter a Native American warrior threat was to adopt the same tactics. Benjamin Church, who had understood this before all others, would continue his long military career by fighting against the Native Americans and the French for most of his life. During King William's War (1688–97) and Queen Anne's War (1702–13), he led his rangers to a string of brilliant victories against the colonists of New France and their Native American allies.

The Anawan Rock, in Rehoboth, MA. It was here that, on August 28, 1676, Captain Benjamin Church and his rangers captured the elderly Pocasset war chief Anawan, a trusted deputy of King Philip's, who had fled the camp at Mount Hope along with 50 of his warriors. This marks the site of the final battle of King Philip's War in southern New England. Anawan was later executed. (Wikimedia Commons/Kenneth C. Zirkel, CC BY-SA 4.0)

THE BATTLEFIELDS TODAY

King Philip's War was fought in the territory of five American states: Massachusetts (which absorbed Plymouth Colony in 1691), Rhode Island, Connecticut, Maine, and New Hampshire. Most of the conflict's key battlefields have been identified by historians and archaeologists to a good degree of certainty, and can be easily reached by car. There are also several museums that have collections related to the war.

Many of the locations where the battles of King Philip's War were fought have changed considerably since the end of the 17th century, but still provide interest to visitors. Many sites feature markers dating back to 1930, when the Tercentenary Commission of Massachusetts Bay Colony (1630–1930) erected waymarkers.

The Haffenreffer Museum of Anthropology, at Brown University in Providence, RI, is the most important museum relating to the events of King Philip's War. Other interesting sites regarding settlement include the Pilgrim Hall Museum and the Plymouth Plantation living history museum, both located in Plymouth. They feature several exhibitions on colonial life in the 17th century.

Beers' Ambush	Its location is marked on the east side of Route 63. South Mountain Road, Northfield, Franklin County, Massachusetts.
Bloody Brook	The site lies at Main Street, South Deerfield, about a mile south from the urban intersection of Route 5. The memorial was built in 1838.
Death of King Philip	In the grounds of the Haffenreffer Museum of Anthropology Collections Research Center in Bristol, RI.
Great Swamp Fight	Located inside the Great Swamp State Management Area near West Kingston, RI. A monument there is at the site of the battle.
Judges Cave	The refuge of William Goffe, the "Angel of Hadley," and two other Puritan leaders who had signed the death warrant of King Charles I. In West Rock Ridge State Park in New Haven.
King Philip's Chair	Also known as the Seat of Metacomet, this rock is where, according to local tradition, the Wampanoag sachem used to meet with his people.
Siege of Brookfield	A marker on Route 9 indicates the boundary between Brookfield and West Brookfield, the latter being where the main battle probably took place.

Benjamin Church's grave in Little Compton, RI. Church had been a founder member of Little Compton. (Wikimedia Commons/Swampyank, CC BY-SA 3.0)

Sudbury Fight	On Route 20, there is a marker of the location near the intersection with Concord Road.
Turner's Falls	Located at the intersection between Montague City Road and French King Highway, north of present-day Montague.
Wheeler's Surprise	On Route 67, its location is marked near Thompson Road.

BIBLIOGRAPHY

Primary sources

Church, Benjamin, *The Entertaining History of King Philip's War*, Boston, 1716

Hubbard, William, *The History of Indian Wars in New England*, Boston, 1677

Mather, Increase, *The History of King Philip's War*, Boston, 1676

Rowlandson, Mary, *The Narrative of the Captivity and Restoration of Mrs. Mary Rowlandson*, Boston, 1682

Secondary sources

Adams, James Truslow, *The Founding of New England*, The Atlantic Monthly Press, 1921

Bodge, George Madison, *Soldiers in King Philip's War*, David Clapp and Son, 1906

Calloway, Colin, *After King Philip's War*, Dartmouth College Press, 1997

Chartrand, René, *Canadian Military Heritage*, vol. 1: *1000–1754*, Art Global, 1993

——, *Colonial American Troops 1610–1774 (2)*, Osprey Publishing Ltd., 2002

Drake, James David, *King Philip's War: Civil War in New England 1675–1676*, University of Massachusetts Press, 2000

Ellis, George W., and Morris, John E., *King Philip's War*, Grafton Press, 1906

Esposito, Gabriele, *Armies of Early Colonial America 1607–1714*, Pen & Sword, 2018

Gallay, Allan, *Colonial Wars of North America 1512–1763: An Encyclopedia*, Routledge, 1996

Johnson, Michael G., *American Woodland Indians*, Osprey Publishing Ltd., 1990

——, *Tribes of the Iroquois Confederacy*, Osprey Publishing Ltd., 2003

——, *Indian Tribes of the New England Frontier*, Osprey Publishing Ltd., 2006

——, *North American Indian Tribes of the Great Lakes*, Osprey Publishing Ltd., 2011

Leach, Douglas Edward, *Flintlock and Tomahawk: New England in King Philip's War*, Macmillan, 1958

——, *Arms for Empire: A Military History of the British Colonies in North America 1607–1763*, Macmillan, 1973

Lepore, Jill, *The Name of War: King Philip's War and the Origins of American Identity*, Knopf, 1998

Mandell, Daniel R., *Behind the Frontier*, University of Nebraska Press, 1996

Malone, Patrick, *The Skulking Way of War*, Madison Books, 1991

Nellis, Eric, *An Empire of Regions: A Brief History of Colonial British America*, University of Toronto Press, 2010

Peterson, Harold L., *Arms and Armor in Colonial America 1526–1783*, Stackpole Company, 1956

Puglisi, Michael J., *Puritans Besieged*, University Press of America, 1991

Schultz, Eric B., and Tougias, Michael J., *King Philip's War: The History and Legacy of America's Forgotten Conflict*, The Countryman Press, 1999

Slotkin, Richard, and Folson, James K., *So Dreadful a Judgement: Puritan Responses to King Philip's War 1675–1676*, Wesleyan University Press, 1978

Tisdale, Donald A., *Soldiers of the Virginia Colony 1607–1699*, Dietz, 2000

Ward, Harry M., *The United Colonies of New England 1643–1690*, Vantage Press, 1961

Weeden, William Babcock, *Economic and Social History of New England, 1620–1789*, The Universide Press, 1890

Windrow, Martin, *Military Dress of North America 1660–1970*, Scribner, 1973

Zaboly, Gary, *American Colonial Ranger*, Osprey Publishing Ltd., 2004

INDEX

Figures in **bold** refer to illustrations.

Abbadie de Saint-Castin, Jean-Vincent
  d' 54
Abenaki peoples 6, 8–9, 39, 54–56, 90
Agawam tribe 63
Alderman, John **89**, 90
Anawan Rock **91**
Andros, Edmund 73
Androscoggin nation 6, 54
Appleton, Major Samuel 64, 68–69
Army of the United Provinces 65–73
artillery 36
Avery, Captain James 68–69

Beers, Captain Richard 53–54, 55,
  56–57
Beers' Ambush (1675) **55**, 56–61, **57**, 92
Block Island 14
Bloody Brook, Battle of (1675) **58–59**,
  61–62, **61**, **62**, 92
Bobbettre, Albert, engravings by **9**
Boston, Paul Revere House 38
Bradford, Major William, Jr. 68–69
  journal 8
Bridgewater 84
Brocklebank, Captain Samuel 78, 82,
  83–84
Brookfield, Siege of (1675) 49–53,
  50–51, **52**, 92

Calvert, George 18
Canonchet 26, 65–66, 79, 81–82
Cape Ann 10–12
Carolina 19
Carver, John 8
Casco, Treaty of (1678) 90
Cassacinamon 81
cavalry 36–37
Cayuga nation 7
Charles I, king of England, Scotland and
  Ireland 10, 12, 88, 92
Charles II, king of England, Scotland
  and Ireland 18, 41
Church, Benjamin **28**
  background 27–28
  books by **22**
  forms Rangers 6, 27, 34
  grave **93**
  and Metacomet's death 89–90, **89**, 91
Church's Rangers **34**, **35**, **89**
  in action 89–90, 91
  commanders 27–28
  formation 6, 27, 34
  member profile 33
  Native American contingent 37
  overview 34–35
  tactics 28
clothing
  colonist 33, 34–37, **34**, **35**, **36**
  Native American **26**
colonist forces 33, **34**, **35**
  commanders 26–28, 31–32
  Native American allies 37
  overview 31–37
  plans 39–41

Conant, Roger 12
Connecticut Colony 7, 13–16, 19, 20
Connecticut Militia and Regiment
  in action 65–73, **70–71**, 77, 78,
    87–88
  commanders 27
  overview 37
Connecticut River Valley 13–16, **14**, 55,
  56–62, 84–88
Corbitant 9–10
Curtis, Ephraim 42, 48–52
Cushman, Robert 8

Dartmouth 43, 47
Dean Winthrop House **12**
Deerfield 56, 61, 62
Denison, Captain George 81
diseases 5, 16–17, **17**
Doolittle, Amos, engravings by **28**
Dorchester Company 10–12

Endecott, John 14
English Civil Wars (1642–51) 10, 27
epidemics 5, 16–17, **17**

Fairfield Swamp Fight (1637) 16
Fort Hill 8
Fort Leverett 47
France
  English wars against 5
  hostility between Maine and French
    Canada 13
  and King Philip's War 54, 90
  and Metacomet 22
Frost, Charles 54
fur trading 9, 13, 33, 54

Garrett, Harman 81
garrison houses 39, **41**, **47**, **66**
Gibbs, Captain 75
Goffe, General William 88, 92
Goulding, Captain Roger 90
Great Swamp Fight (1675) 65–73, **66**,
  67, **68–69**, **70–71**, **73**, 92
Groton 76–77
Grout, John 83

Hadley 87–88
Hartley, Jonathan Scott, statues by **65**
Harvard College 19
Hatfield, attack on (1675) 64–65
Hoar, Joan 76
Hooker, Thomas 13
Hopewell Swamp, Battle of (1675)
  53–54, **53**
houses and dwellings **12**, 30, **38**, 80
  see also garrison houses
Hubbard, William, books by **41**
Hunting, Captain Samuel 82, 84
Hutchinson, Captain Edward 43,
  48–49, **50–51**

Iroquois confederacy 7, **73**, **79**

Jacob, Lieutenant 78
Jacobs, Captain John 75

James I, king of England, Scotland and
  Ireland 7
Jamestown 6
Jireh Bull's Garrison House 67
Judges Cave 92

Keayne, Captain Robert 36
King Philip's Seat **87**, **88**, 92
King Philip's War (1675–76)
  battle scenes **44–45**, **58–59**, **70–71**
  bird's-eye views **50–51**, **68–69**
  build-up 22–23

Lancaster 53
Lancaster Raid (1676) 74–75, **75**, **76**
land use and ownership 20–21
Lathrop, Captain Thomas 53–54,
  58–59, 61–62
Leverett, John 27, 75
logistics 40–41
Long Island **18**

McIntire Garrison House **41**
Mahican confederacy 7, 39, 73
Maine 6, 13, 54–56, 90
Marlborough 78
Maryland 18, 20
Mason, Captain Hugh 82, 83, 84
Mason, Captain John 16
Massachusetts Bay Colony **11**
  and build-up to war 23
  history 12, 17–19, 20
  relations with Native Americans 7,
    13–14
  seal **42**
  theological differences 16
Massachusetts Militia and Regiment
  in action 65–73, **70–71**, 77, 87–88
  commanders 27
  overview 35–37
Massachusetts people 7, 37, 39
Massasoit 9–10, **9**, 21–22, 29
Mather, Increase
  on Bloody Brook 60
  books by **40**, **42**
  on causes of the war 39–40
  on Great Swamp Fight 72
  on Hadley attack 87, 88
  house **38**
  on Marlborough attack 78
  on Mohawks 74
  on Pierce's Fight 79, 80
  on Plymouth attack 85
  on Sudbury and Rehoboth attacks
    80–81
  on Sudbury Fight 84
  on Swansea attack 46
  on Turner's Falls 86
Matoonas 48
Mayflower 7–8
Medfield 75–76
Mendon 43, 48
Metacomet (King Philip) **22**, **26**
  attitude to colonists 22, 29
  background 5, 21, 26
  and build-up to war 22–23

95

death 88–90, **89, 90,** 92
and King Philip's War 47–48, 65, 73–74, 82–84, 87–88
name 21
plans 38–39
Middleborough 43
Miles Garrison House **47**
Mohawk nation 7, 37, 73–74
Mohegan nation **37**
history 7, 13, 14, 16
and King Philip's War 37, 39, 47–48, 53, 65–73, 81
Monoco 26, 55, 74, 76, 91
Morgan, Miles 65
Mount Hope (modern Bristol, RI) 42, 43, 87, 89–90
Munsee confederacy 7
museums 92
Muttawmp
background 26
death 91
and King Philip's War 48–53, **58–59,** 62, 83
Mystic Massacre (1637) 16, 39

Narragansett confederacy
commanders 26
history 7, 13, 14, 16
and King Philip's War 39, 40, 43, 65–73, **70–71,** 74–75, 77, 78–80, 81–82
relations with Wampanoags 21
Nashaway nation 7, 26, 39, 55, 79
Native American forces **26**
allies to colonists 37
commanders 26, 29
overview 29–31
plans 38–39
Native Americans
allied to English 5–6, 34, 37
disease epidemics 17, **17**
in and around New England 6–7, 39
overview 5
relations with colonists 8–10, 12–16, 19–23
settlements **29, 39**
see also individual peoples by name
Netherlands 5, 8, 22
New England
colonists' life 5
history 5, 6–23
maps **4, 6, 14, 18, 20**
population sizes 39
settlement pattern 5
New England Confederation 17–18
New Hampshire Colony 12–13
militia man **36**
New Haven Colony 13
New York (formerly New Netherland) 7, **18,** 19, 73
Newbury, Captain Benjamin 87
Newport 16
Niantic people 7, 13–14, 37, 39, 81
Nipmuc nations
commanders 26
history 7
and King Philip's War 39, 40, 42, 43, 48–53, **58–59,** 62, 67, 74–77, 79
Nipsachuc, Battle of (1675) 47–48

Northampton 77
Northfield **55,** 56–61
Norwottuck nation 7, 39, 53–54

Oaks, Captain Edward 75
Old Rehoboth 43, 47, 81
Oldham, John 14
Oneida nation 7
Oneko 37, 47, 73, 81
Onondaga nation 7

Pequot nation 7, 39, 69, 81
Pequot War (1636–38) 13–16
Peter (Native American ally) 65–66, 67
Philip, King *see* Metacomet
Philips, Major William 54
Pierce, Captain Michael 78–80
Pierce's Fight (1676) 78–80
Pilgrim Fathers 7–10
Plymouth 85
Plymouth Colony **6, 15**
and build-up to war 23
history 7–10, 18, 19, 20, 21, 22
seal **77**
Plymouth Militia 26–27, 33–34, 65–73, **70–71**
Pocasset Country 43–47
Pocumtuc confederacy 7, 55, 73
Podunk people 7, 39, 79
Portsmouth 16
Powhatan confederacy 5
Praying Indians 37, 39
Providence, RI 43, 81
Providence Plantation 16
Puritans *see* religion
Pynchon, William **63,** 64

Rasieres, Isaack de 33–34
religion
Catholic colonies 18
as cause of conflict with Native Americans 19–20
as cause of migration to America 6, 7–8, 10
Charles II tries to control colonial 18
Christian Native Americans 19, 21, **42**
and colonists' response to the war 39–40
theological differences in Massachusetts 16
Revere, Paul, engravings by **28**
Rhode Island Colony 7, **15,** 16, 19, 20, 43, 81
Rice, Edmund, house 80
Rowlandson, Joseph 74, 75
Rowlandson, Mary 74, 75, 76, 82–83, 84

Saco River 54–56
Salem 10, 12
Salsbury, William **44–45**
Samoset 8–9
Sassamon, John 19, 23
Savage, Major Thomas 43, 47
Saybrook Colony 13, 14–16
Scituate 82
Seller, John, maps by **14**
Seneca nation 7

settlements, Native American **29, 39**
Smith's Castle 65, **66**
Sokoki nation 6, 54
Springfield, Siege of (1675) 63–64, **63, 65**
Squanto 8–9, 54
Standish, Myles 8, 10, 33
Stone, John 13–14
Sudbury 80–81, **80**
Sudbury Fight (1676) 82–84, **82, 84,** 93
Susquehannock confederacy 7
Swansea, raid on (1675) 42–43, **44–45,** 47

tactics 27–28, 29–30, 33, 34–35
Taunton 43, 84
Taunton Agreement (1671) 23
Thanksgiving 21
training 31, 34, 35–36
Treat, Major Robert 55, 57–61, 62, 64, 68–69, 77
Turner, Captain William 77, 85–87
Turner's Falls, Battle of (1676) 84–87, **85, 86,** 93

Uncas 37, **37**
Underhill, John 16

Vane, Henry 14
Virginia 5, 6, 18, 19
Visscher, Nicolaes, maps by **18**

Wadsworth, Captain Samuel 74–75, 82, 83–84
Waldron, Richard 54
Wampanoag confederacy
and build-up to war 22–23
commanders 26
dwellings **30**
early relations with colonists 8–9, 16, 21–22
history 7, 13
and King Philip's War 42–48, 67, 73–75, 79, 82–84, 88–90
Wamsutta 21–22, 27
war parties 29–30
weapons and equipment
colonist 32–37, **33, 36**
muskets 30, **31,** 32–36, **32, 33, 36**
Native American **26,** 30–31
Wheeler, Captain Thomas 48–49, 50–51
Wheeler's Surprise (1675) 48–49, **50–51,** 93
White, John 10–12
Willard, Major Simon 52–53
Williams, Roger 16
Winslow, Edward **7**
Winslow, Josiah **27**
background 26–27
and Church's Rangers 28, 35
and King Philip's War 42, 65, 67, 72
Winthrop, John, the Elder 10, 12
Winthrop, John, the Younger 13, 27, **28**
Winthrop Fleet 10
Wood, William, books by **6**